The Intelligent Universe Revealed

BRINGING SCIENCE, SPIRITUALITY &

MYSTICISM TOGETHER

Jeff Jeffries

Cover design by Neil Russell-Smith T2 Creative Solutions

First published in March 2023 by Intelligent Energies Limited

www.intelligentenergies.com

email: jeff@intelligentenergies.com

INTRODUCTION

'To raise new questions, new possibilities, to regard old problems from a new angle, requires creative imagination and marks real advance in science.'

ALBERT EINSTEIN

Imagine if the cosmos amounted to nothing more than sterile, stellar objects in the vacuum of an otherwise empty universe. Dramatic, stunning, and beautiful, mathematically elegant but desolate. A lifeless universe and a colossal anti-climax. What a difference life makes to existence, but what if this were the whole purpose of the cosmos from the beginning? How would any sense of that purpose have arisen, and when? Where is the proof?

This account follows my journey to find the questions and answers that connect everything. Not as a textbook for existence but as a book for everyone to build their own sense of reality on firmer foundations. A discussion to expose a thread which runs through all that exists across life and the cosmos and which challenges and expands all standard concepts and beliefs. To be credible, this must build on what science has proven but also re-examine what science can neither prove nor explain.

It all started to come together when I searched for help with my daughter's learning difficulties and found the world of interacting energies. Forces which unite rather than divide our standard concepts of science, spirituality, and even those experiences sometimes regarded as mystical. To know this for sure, not as a philosophy or religious belief but as a matter of fact, makes all the difference to our own place and role on Earth.

It is time to challenge scientific beliefs that come with no proof but, nevertheless, hold back progress in fields within and beyond science. Orthodoxy largely believes everything about humankind and the cosmos assembled by chance. There are no statistics to support the mainstream belief that we live only in a materialistic cosmos with no other catalytic forces waiting to be better understood. The standard scientific line is that just because life and the universe may seem too complex to have formed without cosmic help does not mean cosmic help must exist. Of course, the opposite is equally true. Just because science believes there is no need for cosmic help does not mean there is none.

This continuing philosophical debate has long been at an impasse. As Einstein puts it, we need to see the whole picture 'from a new angle.' One which marks real advances in science, combining all beliefs and therefore belonging to us all. A twenty-first century perspective acknowledging a realistic process to sustain a working universe that is no longer dependent on chance and coincidence.

REACHING FOR A NEW PERSPECTIVE

'We shall require a substantially new manner of thinking if mankind is to survive.'

ALBERT EINSTEIN

Einstein's anticipated 'new manner of thinking' is now forming around us as we see challenges for science, spirituality, and holistic treatments - our three familiar views of life and the universe. Science is making critical discoveries which expose the limits of old, classic physics. For some, spirituality is now widely recognised as a more appropriate life choice than religious doctrine. Meanwhile, healing therapies and treatments with no basis in science are used by millions in a growing order which has not quite found its place in our thinking. The timing is right for us to combine and re-form our three frames of reference as one picture. One by one, we have to revisit cherished attitudes to see where humankind has failed its purpose.

Our mistake has been to treat our three traditional perspectives as conflicting alternatives. Seen slightly differently, they merge into a single way of thinking. A combined fourth perspective for humankind to survive. Not as rhetoric, belief, or philosophy but as a matter of the only fact to fit the evidence. We must take a brief look at popular science to accept the strength of its contributions but also point out its weaknesses, which often amount to prejudices. We can also show where science supports both spirituality and energy work, though scientists often fail to see it.

Traditional science has made massive progress in explaining much but largely distances itself from our other two significant perspectives. Spirituality is mainly observed by believers and theologians, but there is much more to it. Holistic and other energy work is hugely popular but too often regarded as outmoded mysticism., I have practised internationally in this misunderstood field for thirty years with great success. I have hundreds of recommendations and testimonials working remotely with human and Earth energies. My results and experiences also prove how a practical force of nature supports a new single line of thought. A fantastic thread resonates through every one of us and throughout the whole cosmos, helping our planet and all life upon it. A thread which creates an entirely different joined-up tapestry.

Einstein knew something of this. He offered a quote which eloquently summed it up when he observed: 'everything is determined....by forces over which we have no control. It is determined for the insect as well as for the star. Human beings, vegetables, or cosmic dust - we all dance to a mysterious tune, intoned in the distance by an invisible piper.' Human beliefs have shared his principle across the world for centuries.

Although neither science nor organised religion is likely to champion Einstein's approach, those of us involved with powerful healing and other related therapies are perfectly placed to show the way. By demonstrating abilities outside the wisdom of science and religion, we constantly operate where greater modern awareness is growing and where the response to Einstein's call is ready to blossom. We are the sector best fitted to prove how science, spirituality and mysticism can finally merge.

Einstein's commitment to the presence of an invisible piper who determines the nature of life and the cosmos reinforces his advice to adopt a fresh look at the world around us. To reconsider our expectations and look at the controversial, the familiar and the mysterious in a new light. There are extraordinary answers to be found which bring into focus a new understanding of how humankind can best survive and prosper within our place at the heart of our astonishing living universe. We can reach the natural forces that combine and improve the patterns Einstein knew were failing us. Undoubtedly, it would be wise to heed his call for better thinking if we are to deal effectively with the problems now facing humankind and our planet. Of course, any new approach must be supported by the facts and the evidence, ensuring any new thinking is wholly justified. But it is also not enough to reject a better way forward just because it challenges our assumptions. The first essential is to address these wrong assumptions which hold us back.

Technological and scientific advances greatly influence our society, particularly in the West. Scientific knowledge and theories constantly expand, as they have done for centuries. We expect science to lead in new designs and discoveries, paving the way to further progress and better information. Yet we also know science does not hold all the answers. There is much it cannot explain about its own discoveries, and even more, it cannot explain about the fields familiar to so many but which it chooses not to explore. For science not to have discovered a fact does not mean it is not already known to others. Equally, those with no scientific background who have facts from outside science must not be ignored. Incomplete science cannot be allowed to deter better ideas.

A fresh outlook opens our thinking to inspire events and possibilities with different implications for our familiar spectrum. There need be no difficulties in regarding existence as multi-layered, yet we make difficulties when we choose or are coerced to be satisfied only with the noticeable and measurable physical elements. For example, scientific knowledge cannot comprehend why modern companies pay millions of pounds to dowsers. Without having to leave their offices, they remotely and repeatedly show where to find the best places to drill for new oil and gas reserves. In November 2017, ten out of twelve UK water companies readily confirmed they also used dowsing - more commonly known as water divining - to find water and underground pipes and leaks. Following some adverse media reactions, the companies rushed to protect their position. Saying they also used more up-to-date methods and dowsing was neither their first line nor their official policy.

Some went even deeper into self-defence mode with assurances about how several of their technicians had arranged training in dowsing techniques purely in their own time. To maintain a safer public image, water companies apparently felt pressured into denying their use of dowsing. Truth, which was too troublesome, lost out in a victory for perceived common sense. Technical practice and successful experiences across eighty per cent of an entire industry were swept out of view in the act of denial. It is an understandable approach to fall into, but it slows down progress.

Also distanced from orthodoxy, patients in China undergo major surgery with no anaesthetic other than acupuncture needles inserted into points in their bodies. We now have acupuncture centres in most UK towns and cities. They sit alongside other holistic and energy practices improving the health and wellbeing of millions. Sceptics claim any health gains from such healing interventions are due to the placebo effect. A common occurrence in pharmaceutical trials where dummy tablets with no medical component are handed over as though they were genuine medication. This misleading experiment leads to instances where some of those given the dummies exhibit improvements in their symptoms. There is no satisfactory medical explanation for the effect.

Administering placebos is very different from how healing is practised. Unlike healing treatments, placebos do not generate healing sensations for the recipient. Also, clients in healing sessions are not misled about the efficacy of the treatments they will receive. In general, gains from healing sources often go far beyond those of orthodox medication. More remarkably, healers can also mirror those dowsers who work remotely, thousands of miles from the precious hidden reserves they identify. Millions of healing sessions are also remotely channelled anywhere in the world and are just as effective as when conducted at close quarters. The healing practitioners and their clients do not have to be in the same country to enjoy a physical and direct healing impact. Such experiences have been around for thousands of years, offering help to millions of clients and refusing to go away.

Those are the facts which surround healing events. Instead of denying them, modern minds should ask: what would allow these techniques to flourish day after day worldwide? What arrangement might achieve such powerful results? Despite the evidence, traditional physics is confident that such things are impossible. Misplaced confidence hinders advances in knowledge, limits our thinking, and threatens our willingness to explore new territory.

We know the planet has an abundance of plants thought to have healing properties and contain chemicals which now form the basis of powerful pharmaceutical medication for both ancient and current ailments. Scientists have also suggested there are thousands of potential antibiotic treatments to be farmed from microbes in the Earth's soil. Microbes pre-date us by about 4 billion years, yet they hold promise for the advanced medication desperately required in human society.

Nature surrounds us with healing and life-saving treatments which benefit the health of humankind from long before we appeared on the planet. Rather than being a coincidence, this reads as evidence to support the comments of theoretical physicist Freeman Dyson, who said: 'The more I examine the universe and study the details of its architecture, the more evidence I find that the universe in some sense must have known we were coming.' His words chime nicely with those of Einstein, whose 'invisible piper' is a metaphor for something far more natural - an overarching power offering clues and evidence to reveal an entirely new world. A world waiting for us with much more than healing plants at our disposal.

Surveys constantly reveal how over fifty per cent of those surveyed believe there is more to life and the universe than traditional scientific thinking allows. This often confounds those who cannot see why so many of us no longer entirely accept the scientific lead. At the same time, the sceptics continue to place credence in their only available option of chance to account for the vitally sophisticated progression we now see as the universe.

Dismissing any other possibility but coincidence behind the universe is not just mistaken. It causes us to ignore credible and vitally important influences already making unsung differences in our lives every day and with hidden messages to be shared.

FINDING THE PATH

'The only source of knowledge is experience.'

ALBERT EINSTEIN

I was not always so certain that science was missing the point so badly. In my earlier days, I had no regard for what might have seemed the supernatural until I directly 'experienced knowledge' as observed by Einstein. Personal experiences showed me how common sense offers useful points of view but without evidence or facts to support them. It floats opinions that encourage many to doubt events familiar to millions but which common sense cannot reconcile. In truth, inspired and limitless ways of thinking beyond common sense have always been the path to real progress. In the 1990s, I unexpectedly found this new world through a newspaper feature about a healer based in London.

The article described how the journalist was impressed when the healer showed her how she carried out healing work with clients. It included a case study about the successful treatment of a client suffering from myalgic encephalomyelitis (M.E.). The journalist also wrote she felt physical sensations during a demonstration when the healer put her hands close to her body. To the journalist's amazement, the healer could then accurately diagnose her specific health issues, not having previously been told about any of her conditions.

No doubt most readers of that article would turn the page and move on, but my wife and I had reason to look more closely at the healer's abilities. We desperately hoped something could be done for our ten-year-old daughter Jenny who suffered from learning and developmental difficulties. Of course, we asked ourselves if anyone could really produce improvements and cures or diagnose conditions simply by waving their hands about as the journalist had described. Regardless of our doubts, we knew we could not ignore the opportunity to find out for ourselves.

Jenny could barely speak more than two or three words at a time and displayed poor balance and motor skills. She could not live her life fully, coping as well as she could with her disability. Despite our best efforts, the support available from medical and special educational provisions did not meet her actual needs. Worryingly, little was changing for her, and we could see no signs of long-term improvements. With Jenny's wellbeing the priority, the prospect of a healing intervention seemed heaven-sent. When we met the healer, she confirmed how she would pass her hands over and around Jenny, approximately 12 cm from her body. She would be using what she called her body energies to withdraw negative energy with one hand whilst introducing good healing energy with the other. She believed this combination of clearing and refreshing Jenny's body energies, almost like a blood transfusion, was the best way to help her body to repair itself. The healer explained how all life has body energies as an essential aspect of physicality. Their role is to help maintain our health and wellbeing. The healer's art is to restore balance whenever anything is going wrong. It was an exciting possibility, but nothing like a complete explanation. It did seem little more than a vague, unscientific, and unconvincing theory.

Astonishingly, the prospects of a healing dimension soon gained substance as the healer's theories and claims took effect. From the second healing session and against all odds, Jenny began to show distinct changes. We saw small differences that were as dramatic as they were captivating. The first clear impact brought about an unexpected change in how Jenny walked with us. Until then, her arm seemed to weigh heavily when we held her hand. It always felt she was at least a pace behind and being dragged along. For years no amount of persuasion had made her keep up; the slower we walked, the slower she walked. However, that day as we started to return to our hotel, we suddenly realised she was feeling distinctly different, keeping up without the usual pulling back. It was a definite improvement in how she was carrying herself. The old heaviness was gone; her whole physique felt lighter. It gave us an insight into how oppressive Jenny's physical difficulties had been for her.

Over the next three to four days, there were other improvements. Suddenly, she could reach behind her and fasten her skirt, a movement she previously would not have had the dexterity to manage and had never thought to try. After subsequent healing sessions, she could walk down the stairs from the healing room on her own, taking the stairs alternately rather than putting both feet on one step. To do this whilst holding the bannister with one hand and carrying a bag in the other was, for her, an incredible achievement. She jumped across a narrow gap between two beds in our hotel room, displaying another new skill. Such progress in so short a time was beyond anything she had shown.

It was not long before she began, not exactly to talk but to gabble rather than just using two or three words. Provided we knew something of what she was trying to communicate, we could understand her better than ever before. Her progress was consolidated over four further visits for healing, with each session involving between three to five treatments per week. Jenny's improvement continued, and within a few months, she managed to speak a sentence of twenty words. Highly satisfied, we agreed to discontinue treatment for a while to let her benefit and develop naturally from the gains she had made from the healing.

By now, the improvement in her communication meant she could make us understand what she had experienced during the early treatment. Jenny could tell us that, whilst the healer had been working, it felt like 'cotton wool was being pulled out.' The clarity of this description was the first indication that Jenny had been a lot more conscious of what was happening around her than she could show. She was undoubtedly aware of much more than she could express. We had not known she knew cotton wool even existed, never mind that she could connect such perceptive imagery to what was happening to her at the hands of a healer. Jenny had experienced a release from her lonely, personal prison, and we were thrilled.

I later found that most healers' clients feel a typical,

narrow range of sensations during their treatment; warmth and relaxation are the most frequent. Jenny's version of the healing reaction was to her as she described it. We were discovering a new daughter and a new way of thinking. Jenny was now living proof that whatever the mechanics and limitations, healing was an authentic and effective therapy. The idea of interactions through body energies became a plausible and fascinating explanation for what we saw. Our experiences meant we had to take the events seriously, as proof of healing and as an introduction to other unlimited possibilities. But just what else could this new interacting dimension do?

There was an obvious link between what little I knew of water divining - which I was persuaded to call dowsing - and the healing we had witnessed. Both relied on some form of interacting energies to affect our bodies in ways which defied rational explanations. In one case, health was improved, and in the other, signals passed on information. To the sceptic, the dowsing technique (still practised by water companies and others) is an even less likely concept than healing. The healer opened us up to this twist by asking if we lived anywhere near running water or mine workings. She wanted to determine by dowsing if those features were related to Jenny's learning difficulties. We did live near former mine workings, which meant there would be underground running water, but it was not clear how this could be connected to her problems. It turned out the point of the question was to establish whether something called geopathic stress was having an effect.

I now know geopathic stress happens once the

Earth's magnetic field is distorted underground as it passes through streams and other features. It is believed this creates a weak magnetic influence that disturbs the wavelength of the Earth's natural magnetism, making it incompatible with those body energies on which we all rely and with which healers work. Geopathic stress rises to the Earth's surface and beyond. The magnetism passes through land and property in its adverse state to affect life forms in its path, disturbing and inhibiting the ability of our body energies to work properly. It creates an interference leading to health issues that can take any form but might easily include a learning difficulty. Quite a revelation for us, but how would dowsing help?

I quickly discovered dowsers seek and gather information through dowsing rods which cross over each other, sometimes dipping or rising. The dowsers mentally focus on the issues they wish to establish by asking questions which can be answered by either yes or no. The responses are signalled as answers through impulsive muscle movements, which are exaggerated by how the rods move. The movements differ according to whether the muscular reaction to the question is positive or negative: yes or no. More convenient than using rods is to use a pendulum, a weight on the end of a thread, which in the hands of the dowser, swings or spins to indicate a similar positive or negative reaction to the dowser's questions. Those with the ability can readily interpret findings not otherwise available without specialist equipment and much more effort. Some can find answers not available at all - such as the whereabouts of those oil and gas reserves.

Dowsing is a much more widespread practice than

is generally realised. The American Society of Dowers, and the British Society, have many thousands of registered members. Their numbers reflect only a tiny proportion of those who practise the skill; a vast group of people in two western countries carry out dowsing precisely because they know it works. Many do it professionally and have clients who use their services repeatedly.

In modern times, dowsing has been used for decades, but we can look back over hundreds, or even thousands of years, to find its equivalent amongst our ancestors. The journal of the American Society of Dowsers once reminded its readership how in times past, rulers and leaders turned to dowsers when needing information. They were responsible for planning for and guiding their people, particularly in finding water supplies in a mutual arrangement which could make or break both parties. Wrong information leading to bad decisions could mean execution for the dowsers and, at the very least, loss of power for the unsuccessful leaders.

It has been an accepted technique used by engineers in the British Army and the American military. Members of the Royal Engineers set up the British Society of Dowsers. Some years ago, volunteer dowsers helped find and restore underground facilities connected to the First World War. They detected trenches at Flanders nearly a century after the Great War ended. Even so, because the art is inexplicable to science and requires an aptitude on the part of individual dowsers, it remains controversial.

Dowsing may have no basis in science, but it is not

a fringe activity. Nor is it only used on odd occasions behind the scenes by a few enlightened organisations. It is also used by members of the public who are aware of its value. When I was a child, I discovered my uncle had a recognised ability to detect the sex of a foetus by pendulum dowsing over the tummy of the mother-to-be. Tradespeople also use the technique, as I learned from a sceptical friend. A plumber had called to fix a broken drain for his neighbour and began crisscrossing the area with dowsing rods. He soon located the underground breach before digging to expose the problem, fixing it, and going on his way without fuss. The telling feature is not that the plumber successfully dowsed, but that he regularly used the process as a natural part of his work. He relied on it to save him from wasted time and effort. He did it because he could, despite science.

From the ancients to modern entrepreneurs and those technicians in water companies, dowsing has been employed repeatedly. The practice would not have spread or continued to the present day if it did not keep delivering the results. Even so, dowsing and those who believe in or practise it are often mocked by sceptics. As with healing, the easy assumption is that there can be no means by which it can exist as a natural process. Those who involve themselves are considered to be under some delusion, and therefore their skills are unacknowledged.

In fact, the practitioners, no matter what their background, are generally intelligent and articulate. Articles in dowsing journals impressively carry solid evidence written by enlightened members, often with backgrounds in science, engineering, mathematics, teaching, and medicine. These credentials do not necessarily carry much weight with the sceptics who often claim that past experimental trials have either disproved dowsing results or found them to be no better than chance, especially (they say) considering how underground watercourses could be found almost anywhere. It is a response which takes no account of the facts. It ignores how dowsers successfully gather accurate information on underground streams' depth and flow rates, as well as topics not connected to running water, and how the movement of rods and pendulums varies to reflect the information being conveyed. Those water company engineers and the dowsers who find pipes, oil, and other reserves regularly expose the myths about dowsing trials.

Staged trials of dowsing can become unreliable when they are conducted in ways which interfere with dowsing in practice. A dowser working normally simply focuses on the art of dowsing, but under the duress of a test, there are other distractions. Quantum physics recognises that observing particles makes them behave differently from when they are not being observed. A principle which could easily be extended to energy interactions during dowsing. Partaking in trials, as opposed to their regular day-to-day dowsing, would introduce stress for the dowser, which could also interfere with the results.

Meanwhile, there are thousands of cases where

dowsing is proven effective.[1] Compelling independent evidence of dowsing is shown in a DVD on my website featuring Clive Anderson, an initially sceptical U.K. television personality discovering his own ability to dowse with rods. His body language and the shock on his face should be required viewing for all those who think they know better.

Both healing and dowsing carried out remotely to and from anywhere in the world produce results through the common thread of energies. Body energies link Jenny's improved health, the idea of geopathic stress as an adverse influence on her, and the art of dowsing to find it. Making these connections and adjusting to their implications is richly inspiring. It encourages open and inquiring minds to examine new possibilities and opportunities.

Body energies are easy to establish. Virtually all the material available has something in common to say about them. Many different therapies and techniques work through the same broad mechanism of body energies as a practical component of all human, animal and plant structures. Intriguingly, the body energy system even matches the physiology generally familiar

---

[1] There is a vast collection of energy work information in books, many other publications, and on the internet. It shows the widespread interest in and knowledge of interactive energies worldwide. The British and the American Societies of Dowsers stock publications covering the topics of dowsing and Earth energies as well as other related themes. Richard Creightmore, M.A. (Oxon), B.Ac is an authority on interactive Earth energies, with a wealth of material in his name available via the internet. The Geomancy Group website carries a definitive article, including an extensive bibliography, which traces an understanding of negative Earth energies back to the Chinese Emperor Kuang Yu, who ruled from 2205 BC to 2197 BC.

to everyone. The energy version is a critical, interactive, and practical feature made up of:

An energy mass is sometimes known as the aura. It is the energy equivalent of the overall physical form of the body, a mass of energy throughout every physical frame and extending beyond it. Some energy workers can see the human energy field outside the body. They use their own gift to analyse health issues from its colours and condition. The energy mass is claimed to comprise seven distinct levels and is relatively easy to feel for ourselves.

Energy centres are more commonly known as chakras. They can be regarded as reflecting our major organs and endocrine system. There are said to be at least seven major body chakras running from a point just above the top of the head down the body via the area of the forehead, the throat, the centre of the chest, the solar plexus, and the lower abdomen to the base of the spine. These seven chakras, too, reach beyond and around our physical bodies. There are also said to be minor chakras in each of our joints, plus additional, major out-of-body ones outside our physical frame.

Energy flows run along channels and meridians throughout the body in much the same way as the lines of our blood circulation, lymphatic, and nervous systems. The energy flows are manipulated with needles in acupuncture to achieve healings and pain relief. In the spring of 2009, NICE (the U.K.'s National Institute for Clinical Excellence) recommended acupuncture as a bona fide treatment, but with zero knowledge of how it works. Reflexology, acupressure, and some forms of massage also tap into these channels.

A big step to becoming more comfortable about the presence of body energies is to test whether you sense them for yourself. To do this, relax and hold your hands out in front of you with your palms facing one another, and your elbows bent as if ready to clap. Imagine electricity flying between your hands for a few seconds; you may feel a tingling sensation. Whether or not you do feel anything at this point, start to bring your hands together and then apart again, as if playing an imaginary concertina. Hold them close without their touching and move them gently in and out. After a few seconds, you may gain a sense of warmth or tingling and the feel of a magnetic pulling or pushing growing between your hands. Anything you detect like this is your energy field. About one in four people can get a reaction the first time. If you are not immediately receptive, do keep trying. It may help to invite friends or family to experiment as well. Sooner or later, you will experience confirmation that the body energies do exist, which supports the contention that their purpose is to enable healing.

Once you can feel your body energies that way, try to feel the body energies of other people. With their permission, slowly walk towards them until you can feel the same tingling energy you felt with your own. This tells you how far their body energy field extends beyond their physical frame. Now ask them to think of something positive or sad and check how far their field extends. Within a few seconds, you should find the point at which you can feel their energy has changed. Using this to experiment, you can tell that when they are thinking troubling or negative thoughts, their energy will be closer to their body than when they are thinking positively. The change shows how negativity tightens our energies, making them less effective. When a person is in a positive frame, their energy field is extended and open, but their body energy state is adversely affected by any mental negativity. This is all you need to know to discover the power of energy interactions. If you experiment this way, do not leave the other person in a negative state when you have finished. Always make sure they return to positive thoughts before leaving the test.

The key to this experiment is that we are feeling the body energies of another person because their energies and ours are interacting. It is easy to see how healers are therefore using some combination of their own body energies to mingle with those of their clients to improve health, though that does not explain how it is possible to direct healing energies across the planet when remote healing is practised. Distant healing and dowsing require a more complete answer with even greater implications. It rests on the presence and impact of another far greater external energy field, spanning the world and beyond but capable of connecting with our body energies. A vast, complex energy force exists to join the body energies of every healer to those of their clients, whether together or thousands of miles apart.

This natural force of the universe is compatible with our body energies and plays a major part in the healing process. It is the channel by which healing energies stretch out across the world. A similar connection between this vast cosmic energy field - or perhaps another equivalent field - would also account for remote dowsing. The body energies of a remote dowser become connected to the energy of whatever is the focus of their search, such as water, gas, or oil. The atoms of any form of matter also have an energy dimension that can be reached. The energy elements of water and every other atom are accessible to this universal force, which is ever ready to channel energy information onwards to the dowsers' body energies. Remote dowsing and healing both line up to make sense because of this interactive universal force operating through our body energies and in contact with all material existence.

There is nothing in classic physics to account for this world of energies, but it can be explained by those who are familiar with them and want to encourage a different way of thinking. No orthodox mechanisms explain the phenomena, but the broad term 'energy work' does provide a focus. A combination of the body energies of healers and their clients boosts health and wellbeing, often with spectacular outcomes. Having experienced this directly, I was convinced by such a different way of thinking and realised I wanted to become a healer myself. From books, I knew there was another belief that it is possible to receive gifts from the universe by concentrating on whatever we want. I began visualising and mentally asking to receive the healing gift. I repeatedly made this request for a few weeks but without apparent results or noticeable changes. Eventually, I decided to test myself out by focusing on tackling a long-term discomfort in my shoulder. After a few treatments, I was surprised to find the ache easing and eventually disappearing altogether.

My dawn as a potential healer had arrived, committing me to this new energy work which boosted health and wellbeing. Although my transformation was complete, I was keen to learn more.

The concepts had seemed hard to believe, but I had encountered healing for Jenny, as well as dowsing for information and now a start as a healer myself. I had no reason to dismiss the evidence. Everyone experiencing the improvements shown by healing or the accuracy of dowsing is given an opportunity to explore the mechanics and full potential of these new interacting energies. There is no reason to doubt major influences are at work in our lives; only our prejudices can get in the way.

Involving myself directly in this strange field had proved successful. I strongly recommend everyone to explore the practices of healing or dowsing and other energy techniques for themselves, whether as a client or even as a practitioner. There are many books, online information, and organisations to help get you started. As more people investigate their potential and involve themselves, more will realise their abilities in the energy dimension and confirm the theories and the techniques stand up to scrutiny.

Healing abilities within my reach came to the fore, as well as unexpected links to that other mystery topic of geopathic stress. Over the years, my experiences with cases would prove just how vital the contributions of healers and other energy workers could be. One of my early ones highlighted the value of healing to the client involved and the wider health care structure. It featured several weeks of healing for a woman troubled by damage caused by an old skiing accident. Her injuries had left her with constant discomfort and frequent pain, sometimes leading to her back locking and making leaving her bed impossible. A few healing sessions gradually relieved the pain, leaving her with free movement and no longer needing painkillers.

One day she was surprised to receive a call from her consultant asking her to go to the hospital for an unexpected appointment. He needed an explanation as to why a scan of her back, taken after the healing sessions, was so different from previous X-rays. When told about the healing, the consultant's only comment was, 'it does happen.' I understand why he showed no inclination to talk further or consider whether other patients might benefit from this unorthodox treatment. There would be no way for him - or any professional - to see or act independently beyond the bounds of their organisation. It shows how much is lost to our culture, which cannot readily accept the reality of energy work - mainly because science has a different view and sees no grounds to take it seriously. It also underlines how essential it is to break through those prejudices that deter serious investigation of interactive energies.

As more cases and successful healings came along, my enthusiasm grew, as did a better understanding of how the processes worked. One seemingly routine case accidentally sparked another turning point and showed the key to everything energy work can teach us. A man in Glasgow called George told me he was due to have surgery to deal with floating debris in his knee but said he wanted to try my natural healing instead. To remove or otherwise treat residue by healing sounded a tall order, but we were both willing to try.

After agreeing on a time, the healing was sent as a thirty-minute remote treatment to George in Glasgow. That was the only information available through which to reach him. A few hours later, he phoned to report he had felt warmth during the session and was now without any pain. I was pleased to hear how such a physical intrusion as debris had responded to healing in that way. We both marked it up as a success, but it was much more than that. It was the simple answer to the puzzle of what exact features are at play throughout the cosmos - and a solution to the mysteries which have defied science for so long.

QUESTIONS LEAD US TO OUR ANSWERS

'The important thing is not to stop questioning. Curiosity has its own reason for existing.'

ALBERT EINSTEIN

Einstein's assurance about curiosity having its own reason for existing fails to reveal that reason. Curiosity indeed leads to questions, but in many cases, the answers only access what someone else, teacher, expert, the media etc. - already believes. Spreading existing knowledge is helpful, but asking questions of others is not the only way to be inquisitive.

Whilst recommending us to be curious, maybe Einstein was also urging each of us to put questions to ourselves. Discoveries and progress mean so much more when we find the answers within. Our curiosity helps us make our own advances. I had been forced to accept my early orthodox belief system was short-sighted and completely wrong. It followed that science, too, was unreliable and meant my future would be bound up with exploring more questions and finding answers to reach the truth.

Positive healing and dowsing results are a good foundation for examining techniques and beliefs outside orthodox thinking. We can test the practices in the light of their vivid proof of that incredible power traversing the world instantly and the broader implications of a reality not confined to physical contact. We can open ourselves up to events which transfer information and action in a flash across the planet, sharing interactive energies as their source and with no reason to believe that this source is confined to the Earth. Our solar system is typical of billions of others (as is our galaxy), and since energy fields exist here, they will be present and interactive everywhere. The processes are part of a universal pattern which has not emerged simply to respond to humankind on Earth.

Acknowledging body energies, along with an interactive outside universal force field capable of operating directly with healers and dowsers, gives us an exciting insight into a healing cosmos: the way it works, just what it can do for us, and what we can do in return. Once we take this seriously and fully consider what it all means, the consequences are life-changing. Interactions to channel healing require communication directly with the cosmic energies involved. Astonishingly, the forces consciously react and respond to whatever the healer seeks to achieve, representing an extra dimension to our knowledge. To work through energies in this way transforms our sense of normality. To respond and translate healing power into direct and specific help for clients can only mean the universal energies engage in direct and intelligent communication with the healer and the healings.

My healing session with George had shown cosmic forces must be fully aware of the healer, the client, and the start of the healing process as soon as it is triggered. They acknowledge their part in the personal healing event, connect to the client and their location, as well as to the condition to be treated. This cooperative venture joining healer, client and higher forces happens as the consequence of every request and intention by every healer.

Similar interactions at the energy level occur when dowsers are asking questions as part of dowsing. Their requests for information yield a series of muscle impulses to move the dowsing rods or pendulums involuntarily. The impulses are not random - they convey specific and relevant information. For the universal energy field to respond shows again there is a force that is aware of the question being posed and has a direct energy connection to the facts sought by the dowser. This cosmic field reacts accordingly, causing the appropriate responsive muscle movements. It demonstrates how universal energies are helping to channel healing and dowsing results by directly and consciously participating in the sessions.

This interpretation goes much further than the existence of external energy to transmit healing. The energies are far greater than a cloud of power in which we all bathe, more than a conduit. They are Intelligent Energies accessing higher knowledge and with a healing power equal to, or greater than, any medication, either natural or manufactured. They let us in on their secrets and their abilities because, through our body energies, they are with us and part of us. The power of direct intelligible communication is the source of all healing and other energy interactions. Incredibly, it must also be the essence of the real nature of the universe. Sentient energies always oversee and contribute to everything in creation, constantly listening, involved and responsive.

This invisible thread is the hidden code of the universe. All knowledge from ancient to the present day shares this common link. It has the potential to unite and better explain everything for the twenty-first-century mind. It connects those perspectives of science, spirituality and mysticism we regard as alternatives, strengthening each of them. For example, one of the most complex features of life is DNA, present in the most primitive of life from its very origins - but science is uncertain about how DNA arrived at such an early stage of evolution. Also, how did body energies appear at the moment life began and introduce their interactions at that stage? If physiology, as understood across the sciences, is all we need for life and physicality, why and how do those individual body energies come to exist? Why do they connect to the rest of the universe? If the whole of scientific reality did emerge from cosmic energy assembling all the necessary ingredients, then what would preclude there being a force capable of drawing everything together?

Rather than calling on personal healing reserves from within themselves, healers have long referred to the art of channelling or directing the healing energy. Universal Intelligent Energies permit and carry out that process with us. Intelligent communication with the healing force is the only way it can deliver the help we request as it flows throughout the universe. It draws universal healing energy into the interactive human healing exchange at that moment and transmits it wherever it is required, whether by physical contact or channelled over any distance.

Remote dowsing and healing justify the argument for universal energies and add even more to our understanding of the sheer power of this force - or forces. It is time to appreciate the nature and complexity of the powers with which we live, hard though this might be for some to accept. Undoubtedly, it can be taxing to assimilate how an interacting healing dimension operates as a natural force to help all life forms, how it discerns and responds to an individual's health needs and then uses that information to take the correct steps in a display of absolute sophistication. Joining every healer and client to a cosmic field consciously operating through our energies.

All around us is proof that the energies operate in a context most scientists completely miss. Our universe has generated everything in a partnership which began and then evolved creation. The same process now works with our physical bodies day by day to foster health and wellbeing whilst also allowing dowsers and healers to carry out their techniques consciously.

During dowsing, the external cosmic force accesses the energy of the information the dowser seeks before passing it on to the dowser's body energy. It passes into their subconscious to trigger the involuntary muscle twitches, intelligently converting answers corresponding to the yes or no responses to their questions. This transfer is possible because absolutely everything does have an energy dimension and a rapport with the all-embracing intelligent cosmic force. It is Einstein's metaphorical piper in action and how we all 'dance to a cosmic tune.' Universal energies are all around just as gravity is out there, as are radio waves, microwaves, solar wind, and the Earth's magnetism.

Familiar laws of physics are readily taught to pupils in school from an early age, but the universal energies which are the key to existence are known only to a much smaller sector. One which becomes aware mostly through curiosity and self-discovery.

I saw that all forms of energy easily interact and combine. Each person's body energies not only react to other people's energies but also connect to the energy in the Earth and to the energy of the atoms that make up everyday objects. In the right circumstances, interacting energies enable sentient life to have love, empathy and other forms of bonding with each other and with nature. We can regard all energies as different wavelengths of mighty connective forces which contribute to every aspect of the universe.

We are united along with every living being in creation and every accumulation of energies. Linked by particles of energy as one throughout creation. The cosmic energy field used daily during healing sessions is always immediately close to hand. Healers consciously use this universal field, but every individual in the world has their access to the same force as part of their physiology. It is an unavoidable aspect of nature and our place within the cosmos, a permanent contact between the dual-energy systems of body energies and universal energy. The links are constantly in play for every life form. They are there to interact with us automatically, without our conscious involvement as part of the natural order, or for us to reach actively and deliberately in search of a stated result. Healers boost this whole natural rapport by intervening as a catalyst between their clients' body energies and the healing force of the universe. Those healers who diagnose clients' disorders are especially attuned to this healing arrangement to pick up mental signals prompting their instinctive analyses.

Even healers without this diagnostic ability know how a nudge of pain or a sense of relief in a part of their own body hints at where to give healing to the correlating part of the client's body. Similar energy interactions appear as aspects of other complementary techniques, such as causing the muscle reactions experienced by kinesiologists. In kinesiology, the practitioner interprets variations in the muscle strength of their clients both to establish the nature of any disorders and as part of their treatment. This technique is commonly known as a muscle test. It is often regarded as related to dowsing because information about the client is transmitted via involuntary strength or weakness of their muscles in response to questions about their health.

Healing remains the most abundant demonstration of how interacting energies affect life and wellbeing. Most healers sometimes treat animals, with some specialising in healing only animals of all types and sizes. Animals cannot fake or misinterpret their gains from healing, confirming a genuine intervention. To heal animals reinforces the presence of a practical means by which we relate so closely to the animal world. I had separate healing successes with our cat, who twice injured her leg. On both occasions, she allowed me to give her healing leading to a full recovery despite the vet telling me of his serious doubts.

Plants also respond to our energy interventions. We all know the expression green fingers applied to someone who seems particularly adept at growing plants. It is logical to believe the body energy fields of those unusually successful gardeners are in especially close harmony with the energies of plants. This harmony may mean some form of healing or plant care is being channelled by those lucky enough to have the gift, even if they do not realise it. Simply paying attention to plants, often by talking to them, would establish an energy connection via the cosmic forces. Many believe an energy connection helps trees and plants and benefits those who deliberately connect to them.

The mechanism bringing successful healing to us is awesome, but it is worth considering if it necessarily requires intelligent cooperation. Since there is nothing new in healers representing themselves as channels or transmitters to their receptive clients, might it mean the healing energy simply leaves the healer and crosses the world just like radio signals? Is it powered out randomly to connect to anyone in the way of this invisible beam of healing? If that were so, then healing would not have to be guided by a cooperative intelligent source; it could be transmitted indiscriminately for anyone to capture for themselves.

Experience, however, shows this is not the case. In very many instances, those who are receiving healing are not alone. They may share the room with others sitting near or immediately alongside them. Yet only the person it is intended for ever picks up on the healing sensation or its benefits. That might raise the possibility that the intended party has to connect themselves by switching on their own built-in receiver. However, this cannot be the answer because animals and babies receive healing but are unaware it is being given directly or sent remotely. They absorb and react to the healing without any knowledge of it.

Another of my cases confirms how the intended party only receives the force when it is channelled, regardless of their expectations. A woman had suffered for years with back pain, been prescribed analgesics, and tried massage, a pain-easing machine, as well as heat treatment, but she never felt complete relief. We began healing with two sessions of contact treatment. On each occasion, she noticed an improvement in her condition, prompting her to try distant healing for our third session. The agreed time was set for 7:00 pm that evening. Aware of the sensations she could expect, she was disappointed to find nothing happening when the time for the treatment arrived. She was left wondering if this method of absent healing really worked. She did not know that it had been impossible to send healing at the agreed time. When we re-arranged it for half an hour later, the healing energy channel opened the process immediately with the usual effectiveness. Proving she could not connect to the healing force until it was sent to her.

To the ultra-sceptic, that may not entirely rule out her having to switch her 'receiver' on to it at the right time, but it does mean the healing process depends upon the healer sending healing through an interactive intelligent force primed to make it happen. Even if the cosmic healing power could start up such a receiver in each client as it arrives, the healing energy field must still be an active and aware participant. It needs to know that healing is being requested by the healer so that it can respond by finding the right individual target at the right moment anywhere on Earth. Only then does it trigger the treatment, proving it has a direct sense of all that is happening.

Arranging healing over an area as wide as the whole planet demands an accurate, wide-ranging, and super-powerful cosmic energy network. It requires an energy which communicates intelligently in millions of healer and client relationships spread throughout the world. Able to diagnose every client's healing need whilst responding to every healer's request for assistance. It delivers the service instantly for every healing session anywhere and everywhere on the planet at that same moment, showing how illimitable the system is.

My phrase 'Intelligent Energies' is more than a label. It defines the nature of this force which healers and others have used for thousands of years. A force with interactive powers of action, knowledge and communication which fit into our lives, our culture and all of creation.

Reality, as we now see it, rests on two legs: life and the universe. Both inspire the question of how they began and developed. There is mystery in this: theories, key players, suspicions, disputes, puzzles, barriers, heroes, and villains all swirl around in mists of their own making. At the heart of it is Darwin's dilemma.

DARWIN'S DILEMMA

'Science without religion is lame. Religion without science is blind.'

ALBERT EINSTEIN

Einstein's quote is more apt than it first appears. He knew scientists working at the subatomic level of quantum theory were moving further and further away from the orthodoxy of classical physics. This new branch of science is far too esoteric for most of us to understand, but there are a few familiar and very telling propositions we can grasp. Although the implications of what is known or theorised by scientists are not fully fathomed or agreed upon, a more expansive force of the universe to assist the quantum effects is included as a possibility. A prospect I can show would acknowledge connectedness, spirituality and mysticism as well as furthering science.

The quantum and the mainstream scientific models do not match up because both are incomplete, making for an overall picture showing science is generally weaker than is commonly thought. Eventually, all scientists will have to reconcile their findings with more advanced thinking. Not least to allow for how energy workers engage with Intelligent Energies and how that demonstrates the true meaning of spirituality.

Einstein's quote above about the duality of religion and science could have been inspired directly by Charles Darwin, a gifted scientist and theologian with strong religious beliefs. His pioneering work on natural selection and what came to be known as chance genetic mutations to evolve life conflicted with the strongly held Christian beliefs of the time. His revelations put him at odds with those of that faith and with most of society. His scientific conclusions eventually turned him towards agnosticism. At some personal cost, he gave up on his religious beliefs in order to advance scientific thought.

If they had been active at the same time, Darwin and Einstein might have found an answer to the dilemma of balancing religion and science. Einstein's astute reference to the two cultures reflects some of the thinking emerging in his own time. He was leading a new wave - but with no inkling of the potential for energy work through Intelligent Energies. Either of those great men, in their different eras, might have proposed an interactive cosmic power to overlap science and religion. It did not happen, and the bridge which might have brought the strength and vision Einstein defined in his quote never appeared - until now.

In the most influential quarters of modern culture, the presence and role of interactive energies have still barely been noticed, a failure responsible for decades of resistance to vital therapies, techniques, and knowledge. Fortunately, there are many practitioners today who are aware of how all objections to energy work remain uninformed. They recognise how questionable some orthodox thinking can be and how energy experiences carry the evidence (and therefore the means) to challenge the weaknesses in mainstream thinking.

Strong direct links between particle physics and healing energies have already shown up in scientific experiments. Particles have demonstrated the property of being instantly aware of what is happening to a particle a considerable distance away. The proof of this strange behaviour came late last century, during a now classic experiment. Two particles seven miles apart were made to spin in opposite directions to each other whilst maintaining the same speed. As soon as one of them was manipulated, the other immediately corresponded.

The interaction has an obvious parallel to the process of remote healing when it is channelled across the planet. As far as scientists are concerned, there is nothing to create a physical link between the responsive particles, both acting in a related way. They have not yet been able to produce a coherent explanation of how the movement and direction taken by one particle can directly affect its twin. The universal Intelligent Energies at the heart of energy techniques easily explain all these interactions.

Another overlap between energy work and scientific theory is the quantum proposition known as string theory. The theory proposes that everything rests upon particles known as strings, acting as the foundations of the universe. In this theory, we, along with everything in the universe, are made of such strings. Everything vibrates in what has been called string space-time, another way of saying we are all one with an interconnected universe. I use different terminology, but 'strings' resonating throughout existence, communicating and interacting with all other strings would be a scientifically approved version of interacting energies. If we allow for those strings to carry awareness, they are equal to Intelligent Energies shimmering and vibrating throughout every particle, planet, galaxy, and living organism. If scientists accept the energy exchanges that explain unscientific healing and related events, a reconciliation between ancient practices and tomorrow's science will occur. Of course, string theory does not yet go that far and is not yet unanimously agreed upon as a theory. Even so, it exists as a scientific principle offering an opportunity to endorse energy work. A prospect to encourage more scientists to look seriously at both quantum and other interactive forces to review their doubts about healing and related events. In the meantime, the facts show string theory and Intelligent Energies are not so far apart.[2]

Ironically, science regularly offers many extreme theories of its own. Advancing claims which make little obvious sense to the layperson whilst demonstrating far

---

[2] According to *Quanta Magazine*, what used to be string theory' is technically regarded now as 'M Theory' and often described as a 'leading candidate for the theory of everything in our universe.' There are five string theories which work better when they are all combined. For scientists, the theory of everything is not about everything but how to square Einstein's work on gravity with other quantum physics. Again, from *Quanta Magazine*, this is necessary because 'naïve attempts to calculate how gravitons interact result in nonsensical infinities, indicating the need for a deeper understanding of gravity.' As a non-scientist, it seems to me that Intelligent Energies would prevent 'nonsensical infinities' because it is their nature to be aware of and avoid such anomalies. They act at the energy and subatomic levels to give the universe coherence. As we know, quantum science is not the same as mainstream science. [I remain unconvinced of claims by physicists who believe everything rests on 'chance and coincidence' - if they think that, why do they seek or expect an organised process for 'everything'? JJ]

more imagination and lateral thinking than they devote to energy work. For instance, there are many theories about the elusive dimension of time, including the notion that it may be 'granular' and not necessarily the straight line we commonly perceive. Some scientists are now arguing their case for time travel becoming a serious possibility one day. Apparently, all they need to do is sort out wormholes and the right technology. This (literally) forward-thinking and intriguing concept is suggested at the same time as science generally ridicules the gift of foretelling the future, a claim made by clairvoyants for centuries. It is another example of how quantum thinking might match up with energy work.

As an aside to possible connections between the present and the future, a clairvoyant once told me I would one day experience a feeling akin to champagne bubbles coming out of my head. A very strange event to forecast, though I neglected to ask what its purpose could be; what, if anything, would it signify? Months later, and her words forgotten, I suddenly felt a sensation never before experienced. It can only be described as a pitter-patter across the top of my head, though it was heavier than champagne bubbles described by the psychic. In practice, it was more like soft, slow rainfall, or maybe the bubbles and craters that pop up as thick soup starts to boil.

The popping sensation on my head lasted for several minutes, giving me plenty of time to prove how the clairvoyant had the power to predict future events accurately. Maybe that episode was all it was meant to be - an event to offer evidence of access to the future via the interactive energies of the universe.

ON THE ENERGIES OF SPECIES

'That deep emotional conviction of the presence of a superior reasoning power, which is revealed in the incomprehensible universe, forms my idea of God.'

ALBERT EINSTEIN

The topic of evolution through natural selection is still at the heart of debates about science versus spirituality, and it is worth taking a closer look with Intelligent Energies in the picture. How do Intelligent Energies, Einstein's superior reasoning power, and spirituality fit together? What do interactive forces mean for science, and how do they change our thinking? Einstein's analogy of a distant piper is similar to his 'deep emotional conviction of the presence of a superior reasoning power' behind the balanced, mathematically detailed universe. Is it not more plausible for it to have emerged through a superior reasoning power rather than a string of coincidences? Is it realistic for chance events to have delivered: the catalogue of time, space, gravity, the laws of physics (including the complexity of quantum), life in plants, sentient animals and sophisticated humans requiring interactive body energies? Is it scientifically reasonable for an embryonic cosmos to introduce all those vital specific features - and many more besides - yet, unaccountably, to have been unable to include one more critical force? Why not that 'reasoning power' to draw these elements together into a comprehensive order?

Milliseconds after the Big Bang, everything in creation began. All the forces and materials to create a universe full of galaxies started to emerge. An amazing accumulation of features started working together to form a colossally sophisticated universe. Yet, according to orthodox science, the package did not manage that one extra ingredient. A strange omission for a cosmos which contributed so much from gravity to subatomic particles, matter, and life, but no field of nature to shape and balance everything. For science, creation must gather randomly from vital coincidences, all of which arrived on cue, with no means to bring them together successfully. Intelligent Energies (Einstein's 'superior reasoning power') remedy this weakness. They cannot be any less likely than space or time and everything else to have emerged from that same source. Once present, spontaneously or not, energy interactions remove the billions of unlikely coincidences on which science is otherwise forced to rely. Scientists have no reason to dismiss Intelligent Energies at work in all of this. They have their beliefs - their collective personal convictions - but have no evidence to ignore Einstein's sense of a 'presence', he says, is 'revealed in the incomprehensible universe.'

The naturalist Sir David Attenborough once fronted a BBC television programme, 'Attenborough and the Sea Dragon.' The title refers to an ichthyosaur, a super-efficient sea predator living 200 million years ago. Though not directly related to modern-day sharks and dolphins, it developed similar attributes through the evolutionary processes. A streamlined shape that is common amongst fish who rely on speed and including paddles, as well as tailfins, emerged independently to allow three different creatures to arrive at the same response to their surroundings. The three faced similar circumstances, needs and opportunities, and all are reflected in the same patterns for their eventual separate optimum design. If you follow the scientific line three, different species adopted the same chance mutations to begin the principles of evolution to bring about the same outcomes. If this is the case on Earth, it is most likely to occur on other planets that generate and maintain life. The cosmos works to the same laws of physics throughout. Life forms sharing the same background needs and opportunities on distant planets or galaxies facing Earth-like conditions should evolve life in much the same way as on our planet. We can expect it to hone similar physiology through natural selection as it adapts to similar challenges. But can we expect the same random mutations to occur throughout the galaxy by chance? If they do not, other planets are unlikely to reach our levels of sophistication.

It is more likely evolution guided by Intelligent Energies would lead to humanoids recognisably like those on our planet. A prospect which further justifies the doubts many people have about chance being the main catalyst for the genetic mutations essential to natural selection. Intelligent Energies are far more credible as a highly interactive and responsive universal force for the outcome we see around us. Conjecture, of course, but it shows how interactive forces which definitely exist are massively more plausible.

In his book *The God Delusion*, Sir Richard Dawkins tackles the topic with great scientific clarity. He explains how the random changes could generate a single advantage for a member of any species, which, however minor, would be passed on through DNA to all future members of its family. If the advantages are strong enough, succeeding generations outstrip competitors until that advantage eventually appears in all surviving members of the complete species. If a genetic change brings an overwhelming advantage, then those members without it decline, and those with the advantage take over the entire future of the species. They all come to adopt that trait. Natural selection ensures any single advantage permits growth and greater survival in that species at the expense of the others. Those best adapted are those better equipped to advance up the tree of life.

The general principle of minor but significant advantages progressing the whole of any species to accumulate the most appropriate faculties is repeated for every feature of every living organism. Science insists repeated random changes on equally random mutations improve every system without the ability for the mutating genes to be aware of any potential need or advantage to which they might be responding. Statistically, science is happy with these probabilities and holds to its argument that, over a timescale of millions of years, such sequences are not just feasible but clear evidence of the only way everything evolved. To challenge any part of these otherwise insightful Darwinian sequences requires something more than a personal conviction that the whole business appears unlikely. To justify resistance, we must offer a better alternative with enough evidence to support it.

Science defends its case for chance progressions by referring to the anthropic principle. A principle which seems to have been taken to mean whatever anyone wants it to mean. On January 26, 2017, the Forbes Magazine website carried an article by Ethan Siegal observing how physicist Brandon Carter first offered two anthropic principles in 1973. They state: first, 'we must be prepared to take account of the fact that our location in the universe is necessarily privileged to the extent of being compatible with our existence as observers. Secondly, the universe (and hence the fundamental parameters on which it depends) must be as to admit the creation of observers within it at some stage.' Pretty straightforward, and we can all sign up to it - not necessarily in the same way.

In practice, the principle is often taken to mean the universe, as scientists believe and understand it, must exist their way. What they observe - i.e., chance and coincidence - must be all there is to account for our presence on a planet with intelligent life. This sequence, they say, is both possible and explicable. To keep faith in Darwinism, that premise had to be without any outside intervention, and particularly without Biblical Creation. It is also extended to argue that the more universes and life-bearing planets there are, or have been, the better the odds for one or more of them to develop life. The theory, therefore, is that whatever the odds against our presence on Earth, the principle proves those odds must have paid off.

It does no such thing, and not all scientists are comfortable with the theory, which seems to be an attempt to undermine those who argue against random chance. Indeed, there are obvious weaknesses to the extended anthropic principle. First, we have no idea how many planets in the universe do bear intelligent life. The more there are, the more it would seem there was a pattern or structure behind it and not at all about coincidence. Second, we do not know that life is at all possible without intervention - we only know it exists on Earth, and science wants to discount intervention, so it postulates events which may well be impossible. Our mere existence does not prove we did arrive by chance. Third, Intelligent Energies interact on Earth at an energy level and are, therefore, a force which does intervene without any limits we can impose on its impact.

The only form of intervention referenced by mainstream scientists is the account set out in the Christian Bible, which they understandably dismiss. Without that reference, the only remaining candidate open to science is random chance, which the anthropic principle is now taken to justify. As I said in the introduction, to believe there is no need for cosmic help does not mean there is none. Intelligent Energies as a potential guiding force require us to look more closely at this and other scientific models.

While science may be convinced by Darwinian theory, it is important to reiterate it remains nothing more than a theory. There is no proof to support the belief that chance alone is the main source of the mutations. It is still reasonable to question the credibility of that claim. For instance, it does seem odd for the whole of sophisticated life in a balanced universe to be crucially dependent on the failure of

DNA, which causes random gene mutations. DNA has to fail in its singular purpose: to pass genetic information accurately down the line for subsequent species. There is now a belief that every living organism possesses a gene whose function is to encourage mutations, making it more prone to creating slightly different successors. For science, this explains or reduces the notion of total randomness because a part of DNA is specially adapted to encourage mutations. Scientifically, this vital randomiser also had to appear coincidentally. A truly essential feature for natural selection must have been hardwired into DNA by yet another coincidence. This, too, seems to be a far less likely event than accepting the genetic influence of interacting energies. Intelligent Energies, aware of the advantage to be conferred by such a gene, are equipped to help this and every other genetic feature to appear.

The natural beauty of the heavens and life on Earth shows elegance (as does mathematics, for those who can see it). We should expect the natural features that bring everything into being to be equally consistent and elegant instead of relying on unlikely accidental events. We should look at it in the round. Darwinian theory is not about early creation but about how species developed after life began. He mainly based his theory on how birds ultimately had evolved differing and specialist beaks to take more efficient advantage of their surroundings. The logic of this simple natural selection process is not in doubt. However, there is much more to evolution than minor, if critical, functional adjustments to existing life forms. The living world is more than the sum of such individual parts. We can learn more and get a better sense of evolution and non biblical creation by addressing broader developments across the whole realm of nature.

Through evolution, animals do solve problems and make themselves more efficient. The hippopotamus secretes a natural sunscreen to protect it from the sun's rays. The mosquito is immeasurably more efficient at taking blood and getting away intact because it became able to inject us with an anaesthetic, so we are less likely to feel its bite. Such advances can be seen as major departures rather than tiny modifications to improve efficiency and fitness for purpose.

One of the most impressive attributes I know of is how the heath potter wasp lays its eggs. To condense the story, the female wasp finds a quarry, a separate water supply, and a location amongst heather and gorse, which she prepares as her site for her egg. The chosen site for this could be up to 120 metres from the source of her materials. She makes a small pot with both a neck and a lid into which she lays an egg suspended from a thread. She then finds up to 30 or more caterpillars to fill the pot as food, which she then seals with clay. For a complete account, visit Potter Wasps on John Walters' website.

This complicated practice only makes sense to me as having been guided by Intelligent Energies, way beyond the limits of random adjustments. There are many other examples, such as a beetle which survives by achieving modifications far beyond chance. Scientists researched the optimum shape for a device to collect moisture by copying from the finely tuned bumps and grooves etched onto the back of this beetle living in the arid conditions of the Namib desert in Africa. As part of this process, the creature must face the wind and raise its rear to collect water from dew, improving the beetle's efficiency and survival rates enormously.

Over time, the spontaneous indentations must have appeared and gradually re-formed into a more improved state as a receptacle for the beetle to collect moisture. At some point, it must have separately introduced and developed the additional technique of facing the right way with its rear. It is hard to accept how the grooves on a beetle's back, combined with the trick of directing the capture of dew, could have appeared by chance. No doubt the beetle's survival chances improved, but what gave rise to those basic shapes and perfect grooves - and how did it encourage the beetle to act differently, gathering dew in a practice which became part of its DNA? According to evolutionary theory, only one creature in any developing species on Earth could have had any first mutation by chance. Could that really be enough to start a significant diversion by one parent beetle towards accumulating the gains necessary for chance mutations to reach the epitome of natural selection?

If the mutation had struck numerous others in the same species, perhaps repeatedly, this would have significantly improved the odds of making this change possible. Another example is turtles, who can turn themselves the right way up if they fall back onto their shells. Instead of being doomed, they are rescued by the shell shaping, which automatically rolls them upright. An article by Andras Gergely in February 2007 records how Gabor Domokos and Peter Varkonyi of the Budapest University of Technology investigated the idea of a shape which would explain this. Their work resulted in an object they called a 'gomboc', which has the same property to self-right. Time spent looking at natural shapes helped them fix their design, which needed to be accurate to within fractions of a millimetre to work correctly. A mammoth effort on the part of the academics inspired by nature, which apparently arrived there by chance.

Many animals work in packs, herds, or families, often with complex social interactions. Groups such as wolves, lions, whales, dolphins, meerkats, and primates depend on each other. On a much smaller scale, so do bees, wasps, ants and termites. For these cooperative and super-efficient systems to appear initially through random genetic changes to just one species member does not seem credible.

Large and small creatures living in groups have somehow communicated and learned to trust and cooperate, sometimes in a hierarchical fashion. This is especially impressive in the insect world, where those relying on a community approach to existence have somehow formed themselves into those complicated, independent working structures. To set up and develop those communities, they had to understand how to assemble their colonies, share tasks and specialisms, and apply them for the common good. The bee dance, an indicator to other bees of the exact location of a pollen supply relative to their hive, is a complicated system of understanding and transferring information. It is a clever piece of ingenuity, but does that mean one bee invented the code for another bee to interpret so the whole colony could eventually acquire the skills genetically and allow their offspring to dominate the bee world?

The question of how the bee dance originated between two or more bees, with each one recognising what was being transmitted and why, parallels the various courtship and mating rituals found throughout wildlife, especially amongst birds. It is easy to see how the rituals convey some sense of the attraction and suitability of a strong, healthy male appealing to a female partner and how effective that would be for natural selection. Not so easy is to explain how any creature could begin such a routine for the first time and why any partner would interpret it as attractive rather than odd or even threatening. How does it go from a specific quirk into hardwired beneficial DNA across the whole species?

There are also instances of creatures modifying habits or practices almost simultaneously without the opportunity of learning from each other by copying from examples. One strange practice unaccountably spread from the UK to other countries, almost literally on everyone's doorstep. A study in the UK examined how blue tits and coal tits began pecking through the foil tops of milk bottles in different, unconnected parts of the country in a remarkably short time. It is a fascinating example of bird behaviour, but nobody knows how the practice, once established by a single bird, spread across the UK. The study rejected the obvious suggestion that all the other birds began to copy the actions of those who first used the trick. The blue tit and the coal tit do not move more than 15 miles from their breeding place. To have their discovery copied by direct observation by other birds over areas across England, Scotland, Wales, and Ireland is impractical. Referring to new centres and recordings of the behaviour, the authors say they 'probably represent new discoveries of the habit by individual birds.' The report concludes that 'some sort of imitation exists … though we have no evidence as to the precise nature of the process.'

Of course, in the absence of any knowledge of the role interactive Intelligent Energies play, this is the only conclusion which can be reached. However, allowing for Intelligent Energies makes an enormous difference.

In other matters of behaviour, many creatures migrate thousands of miles, finding their way to places based on instinct. Birds and other land and sea creatures migrate huge distances before returning to their native homes. We can see how those who migrate eventually find better conditions for survival. But migration must have started with a navigation system ready to facilitate the return journey and build the pattern into DNA. Homing pigeons are the classic example, and science offers two main theories on how it works. The first is that pigeons rely on landmarks, including motorways, to follow a known route until they are close enough to their home to recognise local pointers. If that is the only factor, this is an unlikely notion. We can only marvel at how a pigeon knows from miles away that a motorway would lead them home on the first occasion they were released. Depending on where the pigeons are released, they would immediately have to take the right direction to fly variously north, south, east or west, and all compass points in between. How can a motorway, located miles away from where the journeys begin, be of any help?

The second scientific theory is that pigeons recognise magnetic fields acting as their compass through a part of the brain responding to magnetic stimuli. This ability alone is also unconvincing. For it to work, the humble pigeon needs to calculate how magnetic north relates to its start point and home destination and then translate it into a flight path it can follow. It is more likely that the pigeon brain is attuned to the function of naturally receiving and deciphering energy links to Intelligent Energies. A natural, intuitive faculty can make guidance possible through nature's interactive navigation system. The same principle could easily apply to all those creatures whose instincts allow them to find their way home or to other locations acting as breeding or nesting grounds as part of their life patterns. Common examples include fish, turtles, whales, birds and butterflies, which have the added problem of flying over or swimming under the Earth's seas with no guiding landmarks.

There are many related examples: cats and dogs who return to previous homes, elephants returning to watering holes many years after they were last used, and house martins continuing to nest at precisely the same spot they left the previous year. A herd of zebras made news when it was reported they had returned directly to a site inaccessible to them for decades because of perimeter fencing. Once the fencing was removed, they returned to the location previously used only by their deceased forebears. A water source they could never have known about.

There is a concept called animal spatial awareness, meaning animals learn their way around the landscape, often over enormous areas. Even if this could describe what is happening in some circumstances (such as those elephants revisiting watering holes), it does not explain how zebras revisited holes they had never directly known. Something else is responsible. Instinct returns animals to mating and other sites as part of a life cycle. It can also guide their journeys to reach unknown waterholes in a process best explained by interactive and conscious energies.

The behaviour of the male peacock spider adds a different challenge to our concepts of nature. He begins courtship by spreading his brightly coloured legs and dancing while shaking coloured discs of a metallic hue. All this to attract a female who then has to decide if she will mate with him. Their mating routine is uncannily similar in movement and intensity to the peacock strut or other displays used by many birds for attracting partners. Across nature, there is an evolutionary gain for the most enticing and flamboyant performer, so that characteristic expands.

But what truly challenges and amazes is that those tiny spiders have somehow acquired and applied techniques to attract females, not unlike those of much larger, unrelated creatures. Again, it is hard enough to know how chance could have developed any courtship practices even for more obviously sophisticated wildlife. But when an arachnid measuring 3 to 5 mm approaches a female peacock spider with his intent and ritual, how does it work? How can the female judge and respond to her preferred suitor?

It seems bizarre for spiders ever to begin these displays, let alone attach any meaning to them, with no apparent prompts or faculties to make mating choices. Yet another feature of life that works best if a guiding force develops and boosts nature according to need and opportunity. In the spiders' case, it is far more likely their biological need to mate was registered by the Intelligent Energies, which cooperated to fulfil what was required. This advance is not restricted to arachnids; insects also demonstrate their mating habits and practices. From the moment of the Big Bang, a natural awareness has been ever-present and inescapable. Interactive energies abound - part of creation and nature wherever we look.

IN THE BEGINNING

'Everyone who is seriously involved in the pursuit of science becomes convinced that a spirit is manifest in the laws of the universe - a spirit vastly superior to that of man and one in the face of which we, with only modest powers, must feel humble.'

ALBERT EINSTEIN

The natural selection process works well to build on the presence of life through gradual genetic changes. However, these natural adjustments fail to account for anything more. They do not explain how life began nor how the galaxies of our physical universe developed. There is no generally accepted process for progressing the physical universe, no apparent cosmic equivalent of DNA or a working arrangement like natural selection.

The concept of a Big Bang is familiar, but there are disagreements about what it means. It works as a starting point, though it is not really about an explosion. It may represent a sudden emergence of what is sometimes described as space expanding into itself and eventually accumulating energy and matter. The mechanics of a cohesive universe then followed. Further spontaneous events managed to give rise to everything else around us, including the intricacies of physics, chemical elements, waves, particles, matter, etc. To introduce all the specifics of the universe we know, the ingredients had to behave in the correct and only possible way to become existence. As with the development of life, the sophisticated requirements for assembling a working physical universe would be much more likely to be met if this, too, were orchestrated by Intelligent Energies. That spirit, Einstein says, is manifest in the laws of the universe. The essential guiding hand behind the cosmos and the evolution of life which must have known its role was to inspire the whole of creation.

The powers of awareness and interaction implicit in Intelligent Energies, or Einstein's sense of a spirit, must include intimate knowledge of that aim and purpose. Without it, the interactive energies would be working randomly. Without knowing the purpose, they would have a myriad of components and potential interactions arising from the Big Bang but with no clues to implement what was required. A random outcome borne of random acts is not convincing to account for how the ingredients achieved a combined result. An outcome which suggests the presence of a code to create the universe. If that sounds too far-reaching and complex for any Intelligent Energies to accomplish, then how can blind chance be more convincing?

Of course, this harks back to the anthropic principle: 'because it has all worked out this way, it must at least be possible.' It is claimed that we find it hard to accept chance as a source because we are conditioned to see cause and effect in our lives, so we look for it when it is not there. True enough as an observation, perhaps, but only relevant if we know there really is no cause and effect. Science assumes no such creative help but does not know it for a fact.

On the other hand, Intelligent Energies are more plausible than randomness. All the familiar balances and interdependencies essential for building a universe and developing our planet's ordered ecological system had to begin and prosper. Advancing all the essential factors to harness an interacting ecosystem operating through the known and unknown laws of physics. The facility we call osmosis, which enables water to be drawn through plants, is one element of nature without which our ecosystem and ourselves could not have prospered. How fortunate is that in the absence of any higher influence? Different plants appear and fulfil their contribution, whether they can be found growing in deserts, under heavy rain, or only after a forest fire. These miracles of adaptability underline how well Earth has gradually assumed, balanced, and then harmonised the conditions with which life is comfortable and on which everything depends.

It is tempting to overlook the vital life properties of organic growing matter. Where would we be if nothing died, if nothing ever rotted away or passed on its nutrients? And what if there were no processes by which creatures live off each other and on the dead material otherwise permanently left behind? Without this, the world, or at least its evolution into sophisticated life, would have turned out very differently or even collapsed altogether. Our experience on Earth shows how life continues to help itself, helps fellow organisms, generates order, and enables the whole process to remain sustainable. It is organised that way.

Like so many creatures in nature, humans have enjoyed fruit and vegetables in our diet for as long as we have been here. Thanks to science, we know the health benefits of eating at least five or even ten portions daily. Without the nutrients, minerals and vitamins provided by fruit, vegetables, grains and the sun, our health would be drastically impaired. How could our lives have been established without the essential supplies to nurture us? Life, in every form, has grown through its knowledge of how to use the vital requirements found in the natural resources at its disposal. In addition to all the usual green vegetables we have been urged to eat for decades, the media is now advising us on the nutritional benefits of what are termed 'superfoods', including blueberries, cranberries, blackcurrants, rhubarb, holy basil, and beetroot, to name a few (and the list grows all the time). Superfoods may be little more than a marketing ploy, but there is no question that good quality nutritious food is vital to health and wellbeing. A bad diet causes us problems, but we can survive easily on natural bush tucker found the world over.

These plants, insects and other organisms abound in nature to sustain life. It does make the belief that it all stems from coincidence seem unrealistic. Chance alone is unlikely to have assembled the dependence of life on nourishing, health-giving food, the nutritional benefits found within them, and the plentiful supply of it around the planet. Of course, life has taken on this pattern incrementally, but it is still a pattern which is essential and far more likely to emerge with the aid of Intelligent Energies than without them.

Many plants can be used as a medication to ease pain, reduce stress, and even address the relatively recent appreciation of the implications of high blood pressure, along with many other health benefits. The healing properties of Aloe Vera are now widely recognised. At the same time, the soothing effects of dock leaves to counter the discomfort of stinging nettles have been generally known for much longer. Perhaps every malady or condition we have faced, or will ever face, is curable by the plant world, either by a single plant or in combinations. Sadly, because of our ignorance of the vital role of the plant world, we are blindly destroying it at an alarming rate.

Compared to the rich life which has developed on Earth, the relative barrenness of the other planets in our solar system might seem out of keeping with an intelligent force successful in populating our world but not the others. Early exploration of our nearby planets suggests signs of water and possibly bacteria as indicators of potential for organic presence. Every cosmic body across the entire universe must be subject to the same laws of physics and nature. Even so, Intelligent Energies have not formed other planets as obviously successful as Earth anywhere else in our solar system. Does this mean the idea of an intelligent force guiding evolution is flawed by those times when most planets have failed to generate substantive life? Not at all, Intelligent Energies do not construct from a design; they adapt and evolve to make the best of an interactive process in all its circumstances and limitations.

They are instrumental in developing rules that apply everywhere, allowing planets to form around suns to give them the best basis for the growth of stable, intelligent life. These same rules have structured the universe and brought a massive degree of order, allowing life to grow in the right atmosphere under the right conditions. It fails to reach its full potential countless times, but sometimes it will succeed. Earth is one example of this. In this regard, the physical universe reflects nature which often provides species with offspring in great numbers to make up for the enormous losses when only a few survive. The laws of the universe offer the opportunity for planets to blossom into fruitfulness. Perhaps like that on Earth but perhaps in other forms, and mostly not to burst into any life at all. Solar systems have spread across the universe, like frogspawn. The one such system with which we are familiar has rules which allow the many to increase the chances for the few, in ponds or as life across the cosmos.

If universal interactive energies are to achieve anything, they require the existence of other reciprocal energies, including the ones in our bodies, for interactions to take place. Without other energy fields with which to communicate, the universal Intelligent Energies would have nothing through which to act. Our personal energy fields are part of complex and powerful interactive life systems. Mechanisms at one with Einstein's 'manifest spirit' and recognised in the 'mind, body and spirit' combination known to energy workers.

Darwinian theory does not suggest how a random genetic quirk could lead to energy centres, energy flows, and energy masses appearing somewhere in the life chain, which must have previously been managing without them. As expressed, Darwinism could not have introduced the energies, yet those personal fields are integral to every living plant and creature. Their role is to resonate with the entire cosmic energy field. The ability of personal body energies to interact as a receptor in this way must have been present from the first formation of primitive life forms alongside DNA. The symbiotic relationship between Intelligent Energies and all receptors had to come together at the very beginning of the life cycle. It cannot reasonably happen the other way around; essential, fundamental energy systems could not appear later in the life cycle, which leads back to the certainty that the fields of Intelligent Energies orchestrated not only the existence and role of body energies but by the same consistent general steps, evolved the growth of the physical universe along with all aspects of life.

Linking the two largely incompatible topics of science and spirituality, as Einstein does, is not a common theme amongst scientists. Einstein's quotes frequently make similar connections. The topic of energy work fits with many of his observations, and this, too, must be put on the agenda to widen our knowledge of what is happening around us. To be aware of such powers dates back millions of years. It overlaps science, spirituality and energy work and moves us all forward - as well as back to ancient knowledge. Cosmic powers missed by scientists inspire entirely new thinking.

Scientists are generally heading towards a more sophisticated version of their conventional theories on how life could have begun. It was long believed it began on Earth with the unexplained emergence of some primaeval soup. By chance, it was struck by lightning, and through this randomness began the process, which eventually led to humanity. Professor Brian Cox once illustrated on television how far this simple view had moved on. He related how current thinking on life's origins points towards undersea vents as the most likely soup. These vents emit heated freshwater into the salt sea water, provoking a chemical acid/alkaline reaction, which acts much like a battery. He suggested it may have been the spark which enabled the essential elements of life on Earth to begin and then follow the process of natural selection.

According to Professor Cox, this means 'we are just chemistry, the Earth is your ancestor, the restless planet is your creator.' For life to have begun around vents in the sea is plausible enough. However, to claim we are 'just chemistry' (discounting physics and quantum physics altogether) is a measure of how difficult it sometimes is for science to give realistic explanations. The phrase is not merely a statement of scientific belief. Deliberately or not, it is a deterrent to anyone daring to believe in intervention at any spiritual, divine, mystical or energy level. It further highlights how keen mainstream science is to challenge the possibility of such founding influences.

The chemical mixture sparked by acid and alkaline is no doubt scientifically correct, but it cannot account for the formation of our body energies. The life cycle up to our deaths cannot be brought down to a mere chemical reaction. The idea of nothing more than chemistry with a possible seawater battery charge instigating complex life is unacceptable to those who work in the energy dimension and are qualified to know better.

Professor Cox expanded his theme by advancing a further definition that life depends on the concept of protons whizzing around membranes. This generates the power that drives us and gives us our energy. By this, he means our motor rather than our body energy. Protons behaving this way, much as a battery would, seems practical and sensible but only as one part of the answer.

Again, according to Professor Cox, life principally differs from everything not living by its ability to control its own energy. Inanimate objects cannot do this, which still leaves the question: how did life start to do it before it was life? A more sophisticated version of the old chicken and egg riddle might be to ask ourselves how life could start controlling energy to make it become life. Why and how do turbo-powered protons turn non-life forms into living entities capable of controlling their energy?

It is possible the professor was suggesting both innovations accidentally arose and combined at the same time (a micro version of the Big Bang), but this is still not a convincing, fullyrounded argument. We cannot inject battery power into anything to create either energy or life unless it has a receptor waiting to receive and respond to that spark. The theory still needs a catalyst to marry two critical components: (1) the protons to create energy and (2) the energy to bring forth new life. Opening a new form of existence with the extraordinary facility to accept and control its own energy.

Intelligent Energies could be that catalytic force.

They can interact systematically with the energies of atoms to bridge the gap between non-organic protons and other energies, thus introducing the gift of allowing control of their new power energy as a prototype organic life-force. Without Intelligent Energies and having disregarded Biblical Creation, science knows of no force which could do this. As an active catalyst for this sudden fusion to create life, in all its complexity, Intelligent Energies make a more reasoned option than the assurance that 'the restless planet is your creator.' That is like saying the oven creates the cake.[3]

James Lovelock's theory of Earth as Gaia, a living organism, also plays into these fascinating intricacies. The planet, acting as a living host with its own cosmically created body energies, would have the capacity to give birth to this new life force. If everything emerges from the Earth via undersea vents, so should the life force and the energies which define the living. Life under the sea and on land emerges most understandably if the material for our life force is also found within the Earth as an existing interactive energy

---

[3] Bill Bryson makes related points in *A Short History of Nearly Everything*. He writes, "Proteins can't exist without DNA, and DNA has no purpose without proteins. Are we to assume, then, that they arose simultaneously with the purpose of supporting each other? If so, wow". [I echo that – wow indeed. JJ]. He also introduces a cake analogy by Paul Davies, who puzzled over how the essential requirements to form life accumulated. Davies asks the question: 'If everything needs everything else, how did the community of molecules ever arise in the first place?' Bill Bryson adds, 'It is rather as if all the ingredients in your kitchen somehow got together and baked themselves into a cake, but a cake that could moreover divide when necessary to produce more cakes.' [That beats my cake analogy, but in any event, we should thank the heavens for Intelligent Energies at work in the kitchen. JJ]

field or fields. Earth could pass its living energy into other potential life forms. Every living organism would be granted a body energy source just as they receive carbon, iron, and all other aspects of living structures.

In this sense, Professor Cox is not far from the truth when he claims the planet is our creator though he does not acknowledge this is achieved by means beyond the current scientific understanding of planet Earth. The truth is that Earth is a living entity with its own life energies which keep it functioning properly, just like those forces which maintain all other life forms. For energised life to have risen out of the Earth means the planet always had an internal energy system ready to produce life and willing to share its energies with the life it created and for which it is home.

Structured energy lines feature in my work and are believed to exist throughout the planet. There is a wealth of information on the internet concerning Earth forces and lines. There are conflicting beliefs about ley lines and other fields that may exist. No one can yet resolve those controversies, but there is compelling reason to see some Earth lines as the equivalent of our body energy systems, which serve a purpose for us and the planet. Earth is better understood if, like James Lovelock, we regard it as a living organism powered by energy lines as our body energies power us. The planet becomes the perfect host, enabling life to emerge as another version of its source and not out of keeping with the familiar pattern on which Darwinist evolution also depends.

We can see how those undersea vents from which life originated take on an added dimension to access all the ingredients from which we are formed, including Earth energies. Through the vents - the birth canal of the planet - the Earth gave birth to life as part of a process ready to be nurtured further through interactions with Intelligent Energies. This is the spark lacking in that fascinating account by Professor Cox.

By whatever exact sequences life did emerge, as well as all its many physical elements and body energies, it immediately had to build for itself those highly sophisticated principles of genetics captured in DNA. From the outset, the genes had to be there for each species to pass on their natural information in order to develop the next generation. This applies to plants as well as humans and other life forms. The DNA of all plants and living creatures are broadly the same as ours, as revealed by the double helix discovered in 1953.

Scientists are establishing just how complicated DNA is and are still far from fully understanding it. If we ignore any input from Intelligent Energies, we have to believe this sophisticated and essential feature appeared at the very beginning of all life as yet another product of chance. Genetics from day one of primitive life on Earth, and everywhere else in the universe, is beyond belief.

In 'The God Delusion', Professor Dawkins concedes it may indeed be 'very, very improbable' for DNA to accumulate across the universe by chance, though he reminds us that does not mean it would be impossible. Many others still disagree and think it is quite impossible in practice. To be convinced otherwise without good evidence continues to hold back scientific thought. We will only advance when science views the bigger picture with fresh eyes.

FRESH IDEAS – NEW PATTERNS

'When I am judging a theory, I ask myself whether, if I were God, I would have arranged the world in such a way.'

ALBERT EINSTEIN

Einstein is typically bold and controversial in suggesting he accepts a role for God in the world. It is pointless for him to have reflected on this unless he believed God in some form to be relevant. His quote is reminiscent of the force he defined as 'a distant piper' and in other definitions, such as 'superior reasoning power' and 'spirit.' In doing so, he carefully straddles the boundary between science and spirituality, perhaps to avoid repercussions in his professional circles.

Even so, he must have regarded the universe as efficiently arranged intelligently. Following his lead, any theories about creation should also look at how interactive forces might have sensibly arranged everything. For life to have progressed, the origins would have to consist of molecules capable of renewing themselves and building chains, diversifying into life. Left to chance, they might never have found that property, in which case life as we know it would not have come to be. Many scientists do believe life exists on other planets throughout the universe, possibly in huge numbers and in different forms. If so, inevitably, it could only progress and reproduce thanks to the same or similar sets of events we see on Earth. This would include some equivalent of the double helix of

DNA (as well as those body energies) always forming from the moment simplest life began. This aspect strengthens Freeman Dyson's quote that the cosmos somehow was ready and waiting for us to find our place. Extend that observation to every planet supporting life, and it is quickly apparent the influence of Intelligent Energies is the best way to have arranged the world and the rest of existence.

At the start of life, Earth had a plentiful supply of compounds capable of triggering interactions which could lead to the formation of nucleic acids, lipids, and amino acids as essential requirements of life. Yet they alone could not create the double helix or introduce any life spark. Even if life on other planets is vastly different from ours, some similar mechanisms must have utilised the same essential factors to develop their version of DNA. Compounds and DNA anywhere would each be useless without the other, but together they create an interrelated process for life. A combination far more significant than those individual ingredients. There is no certainty that such life does exist elsewhere or in what form, but science holds out the prospect that it does, and scientific theories must try to accommodate the belief with something that is not so improbable.

Scientists' anthropic principle as it pertains to life is also applied to the emergence of the physical universe. Woven into their argument in this regard is that minor changes can have far-reaching effects, which could eventually formulate the laws of physics and gradually build perhaps billions of other universes step by step until they delivered the one universe we know and which has worked. Random chance is still their perceived 'architect', but infinitely raising the number of possible failed universes could make the odds for this tenuous process seem slightly more favourable.

However, with Intelligent Energies in the picture, the anthropic principle is overtaken. It is no longer the only possible explanation. Science has ruled out God but cannot rule out Intelligent Energies. Sentient forces spreading throughout a healing universe may sound like science fiction, but the energies are undoubtedly real. Based on the experiences of energy workers and their continuing worldwide interventions, simply ignoring them altogether is not justifiable. Whilst dinosaurs dominated the planet, and there was no science, all the laws of physics were in play. By engaging in reactions and interactions, the cosmic energy force was the key factor in assembling the entire universe. First, the physical universe and, later, the spread of life shared the same principles of evolving growth through steady progression. Any number of failed universes may have followed this path before our present one succeeded.

Another theoretical physicist Lee Smolin makes this proposition in his work 'The Life of the Cosmos.' According to Professor Dawkins, Smolin expands the multi-universe theory by introducing the idea that 'daughter universes' are formed... in black holes.' They inherit the broad structure of the parent universe but with mutations which lead to advances. Essentially the same process as Darwinian natural selection. It seems to me black holes are also birth canals, but for galaxies and universes.

The weakness of Smolin's version is that it does not address the question of how daughter universes take on the broad structure of the previous parent universe without any memory to carry the data essential to reproducing and changing it. Science does not explain how any newly born universe knows or shows how it can adopt the equivalent of natural selection. How does each potentially advancing cosmos recognisably improve and prosper more effectively than its parent or surpass any competitors? How does a new universe inherit or otherwise develop improvements in the same way life advances through increased practical suitability and effectiveness? What happens to the less successful universes? Black holes may be part of the mechanism, but other than Intelligent Energies, there are no convincing means for it to operate.

In another book, *'The Ancestor's Tale'*, Sir Richard observes how daughter universes in Smolin's theory amount to 'an ingenious Darwinian spin which reduces the apparent statistical improbability of our existence.' He adds that a colleague, Andy Gardner, 'has shown the same mathematics describes both the Smolin theory and Darwinian evolution.' I believe those equations work, though I am no mathematician. The same applies to computer programs which have also been used to simulate life developing through chance mutations.

The factors used in the models must include assumptions that those 'possible small random changes' did occur and that they were so significant as to build a series of ever-improving vast universes. There was presumably also an assumption of (1) there being no helpful force involved and that (2) everything could have happened without guidance. I said earlier that science has no evidence that life is possible without intervention. If it were impossible for existence to have occurred without any guiding force, then to concoct an equation or a computer model which ignores or circumvents that fact is meaningless. But factoring in Intelligent Energies as a guiding force would make equations and computer models work even better. Let me repeat, science has no evidence of random changes or that no active force exists. It is merely the chosen guess.

In line with Einstein's piper, Intelligent Energies do have the power to act as the grand orchestrator. There is no reason to doubt that they not only enable living creatures to enhance their suitability of purpose, but they can also relate to particles, atoms, and the whole of physical mass. Making the essential connections that guide emerging potential universes into organised structures. Sweeping up remnants of past ones if necessary to guide each evolving universe as it intelligently assembles and reassembles itself.

In my world, Intelligent Energies respond directly through compatible energy receptors to meet the needs and opportunities of the growing cosmos. Balancing the strengths and weaknesses as they communicate. Aware of all progress and needs, they react to prompts that eventually lead to an organised reality. Perhaps through many universes or many versions of just one. By trial and error over millions of years, energy accumulations plausibly take the Big Bang from a potentially sterile or chaotic failure into successful mathematical precision. A process that is akin to Darwinian principles and the ideas of Einstein, as well as scientists such as Smolin and Professor Dawkins.

When we allow for this helping hand at work in the physical cosmos, all scientific theorising is eased just as it is in the living, organic world. Our presence as part of the tree of life demonstrates natural selection spreading life across the planet. We, along with every other living organism, are made from the same materials as the stars and the planets. This would readily include energy fields which would have first made their way from the original cosmic ingredients into the Earth. As surely as any other materials making up our physiology, these energy ingredients would eventually reach out to fulfil their role in our living bodies.

Demonstrable, interactive energies have existed at least since the Big Bang. Human understanding can only be complete if it encompasses the perspectives of all the fields of human experience.

THE FOURTH PERSPECTIVE

'The world as we have created it is a process of our thinking. It cannot be changed without changing our thinking.'

ALBERT EINSTEIN

This Einstein quote highlights the thinking which was as troubled in his time as it is now. His words carry even more weight because, as well as changing our thinking, he also wanted changes for a better world. Something that is now needed more than ever. Whatever we do think, most would agree the universe, our world and life upon it are all exceedingly complex. For centuries humankind has sought to make sense of it all, yet still, we are left with those three seemingly incompatible perspectives wrapped up as science, spirituality, and mysticism.

Bringing old notions and new thinking together, recognising the strengths of each of those different perspectives, convincingly fills the gaps within and between them. As Einstein puts it, this is how to 'change our thinking'. To do so is not just about introducing fresh ideas, though that is essential. It is also about letting go of cherished perceptions which no longer apply. Was Einstein aiming at this when he called for a new way to think? Indeed, nothing seems to encourage traditional scientists to peer beyond their present horizons. Orthodoxy continues to ignore events which defy its understanding and therefore escape attention.

Professor Dawkins supports Darwinian natural selection and defends the anthropic principle. He has made his name addressing his disbelief in religion and especially in 'God' as a viable alternative to chance events. It is easy to see why the professor adopts the standard line about the anthropic argument to codify scientific opinion. Like most mainstream scientists, he sees no evidence of any other force able to intervene. The only guiding force seriously considered is still the 'person God' as interpreted by Christianity and rejected by scientists worldwide.

The scientific observation of this interpretation is that for God to be credible as the most sophisticated aspect of creation, He should be at the end of the evolutionary chain and not at the beginning. Therefore, since God is primarily perceived as the creator and the start of everything, such a God cannot exist and must be an illusion. Professor Dawkins argues that, in any case, such a power would be so complex as to be less probable than the alternative of chance. Like Darwin, he reflects on the evidence of perceived inconsistencies in the principle of a merciful, bountiful God and life's experiences. These reflections are hugely mistaken.

First, it is not necessarily accurate to suggest the power of a god feature must be discounted because the level of such complexity and sophistication must come at the end of the whole chain of existence. Intelligent Energies could achieve ultimate sophistication and complexity as one dimension emerging at the end of their own interactive and ever-advancing development process. A sequence which takes place entirely at the energy level and completes its journey to reach the ultimate interactive power before triggering the known physical universe. Whether it developed over billions of years (perhaps before the Big Bang or in an instant after), this energy field could evolve into a force able to recognise how to develop more sophistication at every stage of its own advancement.

This new force would go through as many stages as it took to develop itself before evolving the physical universe as a whole new chain of events. Again, this is in keeping with the same principles of the origin of species through natural selection. Intelligent Energies would therefore reach the top of their progression as a vitally important subatomic interactive power, ready to guide everything else long before life existed. Building the energy world is, therefore, in keeping with the progressive nature of gradually ascending life.

The second scientific mistake in disregarding any version of God is simply that He does not appear to work as we are led to expect. This misconception overlooks how God, religion and the Church are three separate concepts. The beliefs and doctrines applied and altered by successive Church decision-making processes cannot be taken to prove a working God does not exist. There are apparent similarities between Intelligent Energies and the power defined as God, which I will explore later. The two concepts need not be alternatives; they could easily exist side by side. Professor Dawkins' comparison of a person God to be far less likely than a universe having been formed from billions upon billions of chance adaptations is his opinion, to which he is entitled. It is unsustainable because it only applies when science ignores possible alternative versions of a cosmic guiding force. To acknowledge the presence of Intelligent Energies, even as a possibility, makes a big difference to any analysis of what is more likely - chance encounters or highly complex interacting foundations.

Mainstream science is the perspective furthest from acknowledging the presence and effects of interacting energies. It would therefore have the most to gain if its theorists and practitioners did allow that Intelligent Energies are no less practical a proposition than any of the principles scientists already accept. The cosmic influence they disregard is constantly transmitting information, actions, and reactions to and from other forms of energy instantly throughout the universe. Exploring the energy imprints of all knowledge and information would help scientists better understand the process of our evolving reality. None of this is at odds with anything general science proves. It is only at odds with what most mainstream scientists choose to believe.

The world Einstein says we have created as a process of our thinking is broadly familiar, but if we hope to change our thinking, we must be clear about what is on offer.

Spirituality, in practice, is mainly seen as a matter of applied religion. The spiritual perspective considers the universe and allows for a higher force at work, which religious followers broadly define as God. Individuals connect to spiritual power through mental or audible approaches such as prayer and worship. When seen as the relationship between us and the universe's energies, spirituality need not be restricted to or by religious beliefs or practices. Communication between human and cosmic energies is through our body energies which we could define as our spirit. That relationship is one of spirit and available as a part of all creation. An understanding I have seen referred to as the soul of the cosmos.

Science examines the universe almost literally through a microscope and has produced a clever understanding of the finer details. It makes us aware of certain intricacies, including quantum physics, particles, and atoms, as well as gravity, biology, chemistry, and numerous other fields. To help describe its grand vision, classical science pieces it all together but fails to see any intelligent force at work. Scientists and many academics are generally uncomfortable with the whole idea of any such force, but the evidence of energy work proves otherwise.

Interactive forces are undoubtedly present and must be understood within all three common perspectives. Mainstream science desperately needs to acknowledge Intelligent Energies.

Energy work takes various forms but is often controversial because it remains uncomfortable for science and religion. Interactive energies are accessed subconsciously and consciously and are the foundation for those practitioners and therapists whose direct actions are regarded by some as mystical. Wherever needs and opportunities arise, energy workers use their association with energies for their ability to provide a service. They can usually see a spiritual dimension beyond their day-to-day casework, but unlike science and religion, energy work does not typically explore the broader matters of the universe. Acupuncturists, for example, do not necessarily relate their work to dowsing or the growth of the cosmos.

The three models we have created as processes of our thinking improve when combined as the new fourth perspective I suggested earlier. Energy work is a perfect bridge between science and spirituality. The body energies involved are an aspect of our physicality with robust features which scientists could easily investigate and accommodate. In part, spirituality is an exchange between body energies and wider universal energies, no matter how those cosmic forces are regarded. To change the world our thinking has created requires us to change how we perceive energy interactions.

The scientific framework and a fourth perspective

Quantum science is steadily strengthening the case for interactive energies to be accepted as natural forces. They have been part of the universe for as long as anything else, simply waiting their turn to be understood by humankind. Quantum reality is our hope for the future. Mainstream science is less advanced, still primarily bound up with a traditional, mechanical universe and ruling out any question of intervention by a more expansive force. As few individuals seem prepared to challenge this premise, it has become firmly fixed in the collective western mind as orthodox thinking. It is bolstered mainly by the steady flow of scientific discoveries, which mark progress in their limited perspective. This level of science has been enough to overtake numerous historical practices and leave outdated technology behind. But it comes at a price by dismissing past beliefs too readily, drawing us to the latest discoveries without a backward look. Orthodox, materialistic science does not understand or explore past beliefs as it races ahead into new territory, often with unknown consequences.

Rapid advances through to the twenty-first century have been widespread, with rich insights and major leaps in technology and ideology. Darwin - and Newton before him - were heavily instrumental in advocating a credible materialistic universe as opposed to a divine one. A wedge was driven between scientific discoveries and the pure theological beliefs of their time. Darwin did far more than argue against Christian dogma in favour of an alternative working model for evolution. His explanation was so convincing it was allowed to sweep aside all biblical teaching. There was no room for both views, and ever since, scientists' genius and scientific progress have given science its overwhelming popularity. Darwin's insightful contribution came at the cost of losing sight of long-established partial truths. As a result, the two alternatives of Christian beliefs taken literally and in full, and a clockwork cosmos built on chance, are incompatible - but also incomplete. The consequences press our society to line up behind one belief or the other in a dichotomy that is still damaging to both sides.

Earlier, I said science had the most to gain from seeing the fourth perspective. Overall, there is much for modern scientists to learn and then pass on as new knowledge to help us all change our thinking.

Spirituality and a fourth perspective

People from different cultures and backgrounds will each have their own views on the usual perspectives and how they represent the secrets of life and the universe. There will be individual opinions as well as personal priorities over the relative merits of science, spirituality, and energy work. Spirituality has much more to offer than is generally realised and deserves closer attention by everyone as an aspect of all our lives. It is not something we experience only through others; it is personally available to find for ourselves. As understood by science, gravity will keep us attached to the Earth no matter what we think or believe. Energy work is also made more apparent simply by visiting someone who can help or when we practice energy techniques ourselves. Spirituality is different. It is a two-way process in which we take our own steps to act upon our core being in tune with a cosmic force. We choose to seek out and maintain our spiritual path alone or jointly with others. We do so not just by following instructions, but by the choices we make for ourselves. Spirituality recognises the power of a higher force and is, therefore, entirely compatible with interactions through energies.

Religion as an interpretation of spirituality generally argues the case for creation through a Divine source, although some followers have started accepting Darwinism as the chosen explanation for God's Plan. The slant taken by intelligent design means much the same thing, but without identifying any designer. Science takes issue with both concepts of biblical creation and intelligent design on the same grounds: in each case, there would need to be a designer or a master plan to trigger the process. For scientists, no such architect or plan exists.

The Darwinian influence does not require a god or designer and exposes the limits of fully formed creation set out in the Christian bible. For those religious accounts to be so strikingly at odds with Darwin's scientific evidence encouraged the sceptical argument against spirituality in general and religion in particular. It has achieved a level of certainty beyond the evidence it contains but has been taken for granted ever since. Tragedies, injustices, tyrannies, and wars, some of which even happen in the name of religion, are cited as events no bountiful god would permit, cause or fail to prevent. This line of thinking contributed to Darwin's own loss of faith in Christianity after his prayers to spare his young daughter's life were not answered. However, denying the existence of Divine intervention because of a perceived failure to prevent personal tragedy remains a misconception.

God is the name given to a universal force; organised religion is the practical interpretation of that force. I have little knowledge of religious faith and do not speak in favour or against it. World faiths have modified, shaped, and fought over their similar but different beliefs for centuries. God may or may not necessarily act the way followers have led themselves to believe; this is a matter of theology. However, science should look for the fundamental nature of cosmic powers - including those defined by religions - rather than assuming no active universal power exists. To do so would be to take a positive step towards fresh thinking. Intelligent Energies do not diminish spirituality or religion but help connect science to both.

This means that spirituality, including religion, has a legitimate reason to be regarded as valid modern thinking within a fourth perspective. It is a subject explored and taught in many universities, to which I will return later.

The world of energies and a fourth perspective

Humankind, and every other life form, has had access to Intelligent Energies since we arrived on Earth, but modern society is losing sight of our legacy of ancient wisdom. Connections were much clearer in earlier times, and messages received through the links between energies were given greater general credibility than they are today. Our forebears worked with natural cycles and understood features of astronomy and mathematics. They matched us physiologically but possessed fewer assembled facts about the laws of physics and the related progressions leading to our current understanding. Instead, they knew of and adopted much about what I regard as energy connections. Ancients were aware of how those links reverberate through all of us and how some individuals can better focus them in one or more specific applications. Healing and dowsing are two obvious ones, but much else is related to energy in mind, body, and spirit activities, which ancient wisdom accepted.

Nowadays, many people are no longer comfortable with some of those early practices, but energy interactions do make energy work possible and effective by channelling assistance, information, guidance, instruction, or advice for us to access. Our ancestors would have been better able to benefit from natural energy work. Stone circles, pyramids, and other known ancient wonders of the world are evidence of their understanding, abilities and frames of reference. The constructions were part of a pattern which sometimes outstrips some of our twenty-first century knowledge and achievements. The feats were accomplished long before the appearance of organised religion, but at a time when individuals consciously interacted with what I know as Intelligent Energies to help guide their lives and beliefs. At some point within this pattern, people took a detour away from those direct, instinctive links. They moved on to establish their concepts of numerous gods to explain nature and humankind's connections to higher forces. Over the millennia, the concept of multiple gods faced challenges following the establishment of organised religion and its monotheistic claims and teachings.

Such progress had benefits but gradually became distanced from the early perspectives of those wiser minds who, in their day, would not have regarded science as something which conflicted with their knowledge or way of life. Their teachers and scientists experienced the same beliefs as everyone else. Philosophers addressed pre-existing knowledge and ideas and then added their interpretations; this was the fourth perspective in practice as a daily occurrence. Gradually the early picture splintered, eventually forming our modern society and separating our understanding of one universe into our three strained perspectives.

Although western Christianity has held an uneasy view of the activities of healers, clairvoyants and mediums, there is still an exciting overlap between spirituality, religion, and energy work. An overlap not shared by most orthodox scientists, whose perspective remains much further adrift. They struggle to acknowledge what is known outside their mainstream framework. When scientists form their theories, make assertions, and pursue their advances, they ignore healing energy and the interactive way it can travel the world to help the sick. They cannot address how such considerable forces might contribute to any aspect of science or modern life with all its problems. Critical energy influences are kept seriously off-limits as science maintains its singular perspective.

Any scientific attempt to study energy work appears more a matter of how to disprove the claims being made rather than how to understand them. Science has a role in challenging theories, but scientists should first become familiar with what is being examined. The primary scientific model is weakened because it fails to include a factor within the universe as vital as anything scientists do know about. This factor has far wider implications than just looking at how effectively an individual energy worker performs. The consequences of a weak scientific model are holding back the potential for even more significant progress in health, academia, and society. All are limited by an incomplete picture directly affecting personal lives.

I have drawn attention to the evidence which shows

how energy work earns its place in the fourth perspective. To acknowledge this will complete the picture for science, spirituality and the energy work we sometimes dismiss as mysticism. There is no harm in accepting that mysticism exists, but we do need to stop thinking of it as having no provenance. Energy work and the achievements of those we regard as mystics or psychics also have a place in the fourth perspective.

Already, several major organisations encourage or support energy work, including the Heartmath Institute, which embraces advanced principles and a broader view of reality. They have taken giant steps to produce a major practical example of a fourth perspective. The $2 million operation, founded in California, researches and teaches what it describes as scientifically based techniques to create personal harmony for health and wellbeing. For example, a basic practical approach of theirs is to harmonise our breathing with our heart to improve mental, emotional, physical, and spiritual wellbeing.

The Institute believes the heart's electromagnetic field is an essential carrier of emotional information; that living and acting from a state of heart coherence can affect those around us and our planet. It has set up a Special Care Focus to 'Appreciate Our Earth.' Urging us all to join in a synchronised care series, helping raise the planet's vibrations at such a difficult time. The more people join in with these coordinated events, the more powerful and effective they will be.

Heartmath is also conducting innovative research on connectivity between human consciousness and the Earth's energetic systems, as well as between life forms.

They claim there is evidence the Earth's magnetic field helps to synchronise, energise, and support the interconnection of all living systems.

Other organisations are pursuing similar themes. The Scientific and Medical Network is part of what is described as a worldwide contemporary movement bringing together scientists, doctors, psychologists, engineers, philosophers, complementary practitioners, and other professionals 'to explore these frontier issues at the interface.' The network reflects a broader awareness that old certainties have had their day and that it is time for attitudes to change. It is a far-reaching organisation pursuing the same theme I am addressing, charging orthodox science and academia with a catastrophic failure to see beyond anything purely materialistic. Worse still, those from within those professions who see the broader context - spirituality, energy work etc. – make their contributions despite being forced away from expressing the better reality with which they are familiar. This materialism has come to dominate science and academia to distort the worldview across all cultures.

THE MISSING POWERS OF THE UNIVERSE

'Invention is not the product of logical thought, even though the final product is tied to a logical structure.'

ALBERT EINSTEIN

Although ancient wisdom has much to teach us, it does lack modern insights. Intelligent Energies now have more to offer than any previous generations have ever known. Missing and misunderstood for thousands of years, they represent the underlying powers of the universe with important and intriguing implications for all of us. Active at the grand scale of setting up universal laws and sustaining the natural evolutionary process, as well as impacting on our daily lives. Personal healing and dowsing events, along with all other specialised activities practised as complementary techniques and therapies, are part of this same package. Complementary practitioners depend upon Intelligent Energies in conscious, deliberate and powerful interactions for every session with every client.

But even that is not the whole story. Other energy interventions come along as scientifically inexplicable, occasional incidents occurring to any of us with or without any known prompting on the part of the individual. Often, these energy inputs are not consciously acknowledged but still appear regularly. The very personal and focused nature of any single extraordinary experience we do notice means it is usually perceived as a one-off incident rather than part of the cosmic pattern. But once we look for the connections, it is easy to detect a common thread at work, often in surprising settings.

A good illustration is arguably the most common example of our experiences with interactive energies. For those aware of their ability, events known as clairsentient or claircognizant connections are cued into as required. They are also encountered subconsciously by virtually all of us every day. Clairsentient means feeling inputs through our senses without being made aware by any usual or apparent conscious method. Claircognizant is to know (rather than feel) but again, not by any usual faculty. Both draw parallels with clairvoyance, in which mental pictures are interpreted for their meaning, or clairaudience, in which information is received as a voice message audible to those who receive them. The messages come from the same source and are interpreted by our energies, our subconscious and our brain. Those three features taken together are what we know as our mind.

There is little difference between clairsentient and claircognizant messages, and both probably overlap. They are less distinct than the other two techniques because they reach our consciousness as ideas or flashes of inspiration rather than voices or images. A form of unexpected awareness without any indication that it has arisen from outside sources rather our own invention. Such messages have been received and recorded over the centuries, often showing themselves to be highly revealing. Those we call psychics may be more in tune with the moment and the source of their sudden insights, but anyone can pick up these vital connections from the energies.

The effect is often described as having a sixth sense or a 'nose' for something. Especially if it is connected to a field of activity familiar to us, it appears as a feeling, an instinct, or even construed as a premonition to warn of something especially good or badly wrong. If we know what we are looking for, we can recall occasions when these energies were at work, those times when we may have said, 'someone was looking after me.' We receive communications through energies when twins know about each other in ways which appear (or are) telepathic. It is easy to dismiss these familiar events as coincidence or the brain making lightning decisions based on past experiences before it promotes them to our conscious minds. Modern assumptions confidently but wrongly disregard interactive sources as the spark which informs the subconscious process.

The pattern of 'sleeping on a problem' and finding the answer after waking is another familiar example. The common explanation is that our subconscious is at work finding ideas whilst we are asleep, and our minds and bodies have little to focus on consciously. This is partly true, but the question remains as to how the subconscious accesses or accumulates an appropriate answer when the conscious brain has not. The better answer is that the automatic, natural link between our body energies and the Intelligent Energies feeds information into the subconscious, from where it can reach the conscious brain. It happens more readily when our conscious attention is not being diverted to daily matters. Ironically, as Einstein perhaps knew, science itself is rich in examples of clairsentient /claircognizant information being passed on to guide or help those engaged in research and experiments. The solutions and advances they were prompted to develop account for many scientific breakthroughs. The true source of invention, which Einstein knew was not the product of logical thought, is the influence of an intelligent universe.

This theme could be applied to most, if not all, those who have moved life along in any giant leap in science, literature, art or other fields. Einstein's quote, above, confirms other quotes he made in support of intuition. It is clear he, too, benefitted from extrasensory inputs. In his book 'A Short History of Nearly Everything', Bill Bryson writes of how novelist and chemist C. P. Snow described the conclusions reached in one of Einstein's own most famous papers *On the Electrodynamics of Moving Bodies'* as 'having been reached by pure thought.' Bill Bryson himself refers to Einstein's paper as one of the most extraordinary ever published. There was practically no mathematics and no evidence of any structured identifiable route by which he had reached his conclusions. Einstein appears to have reached them not by a logical train but by intuitive 'pure thought.'

Bill Bryson also observes how astrophysicist Fritz Zwicky is reported never to have had sufficient knowledge of the laws of physics to understand how his revolutionary theories about neutron stars could be correct. He, too, showed no process of logical progression. If complex knowledge or scientific skill did not lead Zwicky to his findings in such a specialised field, then where did they come from? If he had insufficient ability to come up with the theories, the source of his new inputs had to lie elsewhere - for this to be claircognizant recognition is the most plausible explanation. The influence of Intelligent Energies passing information to someone capable of receiving it explains the inexplicable and accounts for intuition as a practical process.

All the world's great visionaries are likely to have had something more than physical and mental skills, or even plain good fortune, to find what Einstein called 'a higher plane of knowledge.' People who made extreme and apparently random leaps in understanding towards precise and advanced outcomes are likely to have received a helping hand from the forces which built the universe. This is not to diminish anyone's greatness or dedication. It is only to say that those who received that initial guidance and used their skills to follow it up enjoyed an energy springboard.

There is a saying, also attributed to Einstein, about success being due to ten per cent inspiration and ninety per cent perspiration. To be inspired is to receive input upon which to work. Intelligent Energies and the claircognizant process easily underpin some, or maybe all, humankind's inventiveness. These hidden influences constantly carry the energies of the universe into our personal daily lives. Amongst the many who may have benefitted is Swiss scientist Johann Friedrich Miescher, whom Bill Bryson says showed extraordinary insight. Twenty-three years after examining used bandages under a microscope and identifying an unknown substance in pus which he termed nuclein, Meischer suggested it might be responsible for heredity. It seems from nowhere, and for no known reason, he had effectively first encountered what was to be revealed as DNA.

The notion it could aid heredity became apparent to him from just looking at the bandages and bearing it in mind for more than two decades. It was so fantastic a leap as to be totally ignored by scientists of the time. He appears to have had no basis for his ground-breaking revelation and articulated it for no known reason. The most credible route for this is the power of Intelligent Energies to hold and communicate this insight to Miescher.

In the modern era, Steve Jobs, co-founder of Apple and an icon of the technological revolution, was heavily influenced by Zen Buddhism and meditation. He knew how to still his mind and, therefore, in my terms, how to open himself up to Intelligent Energies. On the Business Insider website, Drake Baer headlined an article: 'Here's How Zen Meditation Changed Steve Job's Life and Sparked a Design Revolution.' It quotes Jobs, 'If you just sit and observe, you will see how restless your mind is. If you try to calm it, it only makes things worse, but over time it does calm, and when it does, there's room to hear more subtle things - that's when your intuition starts to blossom, and you start to see things more clearly and be in the present more. Your mind just slows down, and you see a tremendous expanse in the moment. You see so much more than you could see before. It's a discipline; you have to practise it.'

This is not just a philosophy. It is Steve Jobs' definition of practical natural interactions revealing insights in different ways to those who experience the effects. The Reverend Robert Evans has the gift of spotting the deaths of stars by detecting the explosion of supernovae, no more than a pinprick of light in the gaps between the stars in a sky teeming with stars. Bill Bryson has observed Evans as having such a talent that he has been likened to an autistic savant. Being neither autistic nor believing himself to be a savant, Evans has no explanation for his unique ability to spot these tiny changes in the night sky. To place this in context, it is a feat Bill Bryson likens to 'spotting a single specific grain of salt against a black background on a dining table two miles long.' This is no ordinary skill.

Again, Intelligent Energies represent the only realistic explanation for the nudges subconsciously guiding Evans. Of course, Bill Bryson had no reason to allude to interacting energies as the explanation for this or the many other similar instances described in his book. Nonetheless, his accounts are perfectly in tune with helpful, intelligent interventions from the cosmos.

We are all open to these inputs, although we may not usually be directly aware of their influence as they are happening. Once we do know the connections can be made deliberately, we have the potential to seek out the powerful help on which we can call. It is part of the power which allows us to dowse for information via yes or no answers to our questions or those times when scientists or others are inadvertently inspired towards solutions with no conscious effort. For those sufficiently sensitive or in tune at the right moment, the messages prompted by the universal energies forcefully reach their conscious brain, and they can act or respond accordingly.

The more we use universal energy interactions directly, the more familiar and powerful the links become. Even so, it can be an intermittent facility, subject to its own rules and with no easy user guide. Especially at first, it is not easy to be sure when we are registering genuine and trustworthy insights from the Intelligent Energies or if something has occurred to us in the usual prosaic way. An impulse with no added value and not prompted by the universal power.

Now I am experienced, I can detect indications that the energies are at work. Sometimes I mentally ask for a check on the validity of what I think might be a message from the energies. If I then get a physical sensation in my stomach, not unlike the one we get on a fairground ride when it suddenly plunges downwards, I recognise it as confirmation of the influence of energies. The physical nature of this prompt suggests it is a form of dowsing, but with the signals translated into movement in my diaphragm rather than my hands. This tummy tickle may well be the origin of the phrase 'gut reaction.'

Look out for your signals that the energies are in touch. Sometimes they are random ideas that keep returning like an obsession and only stop when we address them seriously. This specific prod from the source telling us to pay attention often turns up the other way around. That is, we can get a random thought that something has not happened for a while or has never happened - then, suddenly, it does. For seven years, we had enjoyed attracting and feeding a wide variety of birds. One day, I was struck by a random observation that it was a blessing we had never seen a predatory sparrowhawk despite the area's rich birdlife. But just two days later, one streaked into the garden and narrowly missed taking one of the birds. This premonition of an impending attack was not formed as conscious knowledge of the event in detail. It did not register as an attack about to happen. Only afterwards was it clear to me how my instincts through interacting energies had alerted me to an incident due to happen soon.

To the sceptic, such events are another opportunity to claim it was a coincidence. Asserting that there is no known mechanism by which a warning can be made; therefore, this could not be one. In fact, the mechanism of active connections between cosmic and personal energies is plain once we are prepared to look. The way they have interacted to generate the physical universe and all forms of life over billions of years is a logical interpretation of their role. Their influence is in everything and is always there, working directly whenever we ask and subconsciously when we do not.

Because the process is one of energy interactions, the outcomes always depend on how our receptors react. There are uncertainties and variables in how effective such links are, which makes some interactions slower or less effective. The variations confirm the nature of Intelligent Energies as a living, powerful, natural force, constantly and actively at work. It is not a slick, polished automaton designed to impose its own direct influence. The connection is made through a sometimes fragile cooperation between an enormous energy force reaching the denser physicality of humans and everything else in existence.

ENERGIES ARE NOT ALWAYS GOOD FOR US

'A man should look for what is not what he thinks should be.'

ALBERT EINSTEIN

Interactive energies are essential to the entire universe and life across it. At the core of our health and wellbeing are the body energies we can boost through a range of techniques, but the positive impacts hide a less wholesome story. Not all aspects of energy interactions are beneficial. Some are, or can become, distinctly harmful; it is critical to make this known more widely. The most widespread and invasive form of an adverse energy influence thought to be ruining lives every day is the geopathic stress first raised with us by the healer we visited for Jenny's treatments. My research, experiments and practice in countless cases since have shown how it is a major health problem, hidden yet known for centuries.

It remains out of sight because, again, orthodoxy cannot see any connections for it to instil any adverse effects. Geopathic stress can introduce familiar and seemingly innocent sensations, including simple aches and pains and poor sleep. But these are only signals that geopathic stress may have reached into our body energies and with the prospect of causing a range of consequences for us that can be much more far-reaching. By invading our body energies, they compromise any aspect of our health and wellbeing with widespread effects. As well as affecting humans, its insidious presence also impacts on animals and plants, including trees. Life forms may be differently affected, some appear to be more tolerant than others, and some - especially domestic cats - actively seek out affected places as favourite resting spots whenever possible.

What causes geopathic stress, its effects upon us, and the fact of its existence within the range of energies throughout the planet all take time to understand. Even so, we owe it to ourselves to consider it seriously so we can protect ourselves. The health problems are tangible - and in some cases measurable - even though science does not generally associate them with geopathic stress. The links are there to be researched, which might one day enable science to make the connections it is missing. In the past, scientists and dowsers have cooperated in attempts to address geopathic stress, sometimes producing startling results. If we could rediscover such cooperation, a greater appreciation of healing and other energy-related influences would soon follow.

As I learned in that early visit to the healer, the root cause of geopathic stress is a disturbance to the Earth's natural magnetic rays as they travel upwards from deep underground towards the Earth's surface and beyond. Underground running water or other factors, such as mine workings and certain types of rocks, cause the interferences which distort the wavelength of the planet's natural magnetism. The magnetic field, which is usually safe, becomes much less compatible with our body energies. The effect is the same whether the magnetic field passes through the underground features deep within the Earth or closer to the surface. A continual flow of distorted Earth magnetism reaches above ground level as an adverse field to inhibit health and wellbeing by overwhelming the body energies of life forms.

It can arise at any location anywhere to invade homes, offices, other buildings, and open spaces wherever it emerges through the Earth's crust. It might be generated as a line of geopathic stress or as a pool. Wherever it appears, it will weaken most organisms spending any time at or over that spot. The greater anyone's exposure to geopathic stress, the more it will gather in their systems. The effect will vary according to the strength of the distorted energy field, which can range widely. If two or more underground fault lines cross each other at any depth beneath the Earth's surface, the strength of the geopathic stress will be magnified.

Even relatively low degrees of geopathic stress will mount up over time. Our bodies can soon recover from brief spells but not so easily from more prolonged exposure, say if a bed is above a point at which the geopathic stress is affecting a location. Not only will someone then be subjected to geopathic stress continuously for many hours, but its effects will also be concentrated on them whilst they sleep and at a time when they should be benefiting from the restorative power of a good night's rest.

Geopathic stress is a formidable energy field as it clashes with our body energies. It is a toxic energy force significantly harmful to our health and wellbeing.

Because it principally acts on the immune system to weaken good health, any underlying health problems to which those affected are prone or may contract become much more likely to develop. In addition, treatment of any existing health condition, no matter its nature or cause, will be less successful because the patient's natural capacity for health and recovery through their body energies is constantly compromised. This whole issue is made difficult and even controversial because it hinges on the presence and interaction between body energy fields and the damaged Earth energies. Neither type of energy is recognised by most health professionals, who also have to contend with the problem that not everyone is equally vulnerable. Something not uncommon in health matters, as we know from allergies and other variables. Despite all obstacles, there is no doubt these harmful energy combinations must be understood and taken seriously.

I know of holistic doctors and other energy workers who send clients for me to clear their homes. But, overall, they are in the minority in their professions. Unfortunately, until general awareness improves, few orthodox health professionals will allow for how adverse energies may be acting unhealthily on their patients. Doctors would not want to diagnose without knowledge of a patient's circumstances: weight, medical history, diet, whether they smoke, drink alcohol or take other substances. No doctor wishes to treat without knowing all the facts. Yet this hidden factor, seriously contributory to their diagnoses, cannot be considered during most consultations. Patients risk receiving inadequate diagnosis and treatment because of this unwitting omission.

At best, time and money are wasted. At worst, treatment is being slowed or inhibited because geopathic stress continues to affect us. Ultimately, in some cases, unnecessary fatalities may occur. This is not the fault of medical professionals, who are not yet taught about it and are currently unable to address the actual or potential threats. This curtain must be lifted; society must take responsibility for what is a medical shortcoming towards a problem which has no boundaries. It affects countless properties of all sizes, from terraced houses to Buckingham Palace and everywhere throughout Europe and the rest of the world. Anyone who spends any length of time at a place where this distorted underground energy has surfaced will be affected to a greater or lesser extent.

However, there are steps we can take to deal with it ourselves. A simple temporary way to reduce its impact is to place black bin-liners over the site of the stress, most commonly under a mattress. This low-tech solution will temporarily insulate the affected area. It may sound bizarre, but it works. Because the relief from the bags is usually evident, using them confirms both the impact of geopathic stress and how this strange, short-term solution can combat it.

I have had two graphic practical demonstrations proving how effective bin-liners can be. The first happened soon after we had established a problem in our house. We quickly put bin-liners under our mattress, and to our immediate surprise, my wife and I found the bed felt so much better. There was no doubt our sleep was altogether deeper and richer.

After a week, according to the theory, it was time to change the liners, so I gathered the used ones into a ball and carried them downstairs. By the time I got to the bottom, I felt suddenly weaker and had begun to ache in my arms and legs, innocent symptoms which I later became accustomed to whenever I directly encountered geopathic stress at any location. I was shocked. Nobody had warned me of this reaction, perhaps because nobody knew about it. It seemed the bin-liners had absorbed the stress to saturation point and were now releasing it back into my body. It had never occurred to me that there would be any problem handling the used liners this way. For them to affect me so strongly was another clear indication of how the adverse energies transfer and interact.

The second confirmation came on holiday when I felt severe signals of geopathic stress where we were staying. I developed aching legs, which grew more painful over a few days until walking around and sleeping at night became almost impossible. I placed bin-liners under the mattress, confident they would solve the problem. I could hardly believe it when the method failed for the first time. The liners gave no help whatsoever, creating something of a panic. It occurred to me the liners might have already absorbed stress and were saturated before they were bought, or perhaps were too thin to deal with it. I bought another pack of stronger ones and put those under the mattress, confident they would fully protect me. To my horror, they failed again. Eventually, a claircognizant inspiration threw me a lifeline: why not wrap two liners around each leg, increasing their thickness and perhaps strengthening their protection? The pain started to melt away within seconds of doing that and, in minutes, had ceased entirely. It proved again that the bin-liners had worked and confirmed without a doubt that geopathic stress could indeed be a potentially agonising problem. Because the pain disappeared immediately, it meant there had been no physical damage to my legs - the pain was being generated as a constant adverse influence which stopped as soon as the liners shielded me.

It is important to stress that using plastic in this way is not part of modern thinking or best practice. It can only be justified as a rare emergency solution such as I was facing decades ago on holiday and with no other treatment to hand. Our plastics must now be handled, recycled and or disposed of with proper care for the environment.

From how the plastic liners failed me on holiday, I realised they were not a safe, permanent protector. From then on, the question of how best to tackle geopathic stress was never far from my mind. For many years I have been making my present process to clear geopathic stress available across the planet for homes, workstations, and all other locations, including holiday accommodation. My solution was inspired one evening when a claircognizant message suddenly came to me whilst dowsing. What if I tried to deal with geopathic stress remotely as if I were sending distant healing? I knew healing had been tried by others but was reported to have had no lasting effect. I was hoping Intelligent Energies could help me find a better way to make that work. Soon, ideas started to flow from the universe via my subconscious and into my conscious mind. It led to a system I believed would do the trick. My pendulum and those tummy tickles I could now mentally call upon as an added form of reassurance helped me turn the signals into a recognisable technique which I thought would be effective and permanent.

Having fine-tuned the inspiration, I waited for an opportunity to apply my new method for the next person who needed help overcoming their exposure to geopathic stress. Not long afterwards, a headmaster friend mentioned how he came home at the end of every day with a severe headache. Although this might be associated with the pressures of his job, it is also one of the indicators of possible geopathic stress. Remotely dowsing his office with my pendulum, I found a very strong stress reading and immediately put my new process into full effect. When I dowsed his office later, the reading was no longer negative. His office was reading completely free of geopathic stress.

Later, he told me the headaches had stopped from that first day of the new technique and had never returned. My experimental approach had worked beyond anything I could have expected. It began a new stage of my energy work which took over my life. My friend is now retired, but I regularly dowse his former office to make sure it is still clear. For more than twenty years, it has shown positive results. It is, therefore, fair to regard the treatment as a permanent solution - one I have used with similar success ever since, gathering endorsements worldwide.

Since geopathic stress was raised as a possible connection to our daughter's difficulties, public awareness has begun to spread, and requests for my help have been growing globally. One such call came from a researcher working on behalf of the German military, keen to discuss how their land and property could be made safe from geopathic stress. It is encouraging to see a central European authority becoming more alive to the problem. Hopefully, this is a sign of a meeting of minds across different disciplines, sharing experiences and coming together for better world health.

This is not an idle ambition; although awareness of energy issues is growing slowly, it is now creating more attention worldwide. I have worked remotely in over 50 countries, helping individuals, professionals and their clients in different disciplines. Appropriately, as an international energy worker, I have also cleared geopathic stress from underneath the United Nations Building in New York, as well as many significant buildings such as hospitals and university campuses. One of the satisfying aspects of my process is that I do not treat people or even buildings directly. I treat the planet, which afterwards no longer carries this distorted harmful field upwards to the surface at that site.

Geopathic stress is not the only adverse natural Earth energy on the planet; a further one seems even worse. I was alerted to something out of the ordinary by South African-based Feng Shui practitioner Debbie Fox, who often refers her clients to me to add geopathic stress clearance to her Feng Shui treatments. I first met Debbie when she approached me to clear geopathic stress from her property. At the time, I had limited knowledge of Feng Shui, but through what she told me, I immediately connected Feng Shui principles to the effects of interactive energies. Energies abound in all our lives, locations and circumstances. Feng Shui is a way to bring them into harmony.

Debbie's alert told me she had found three new Earth lines affecting her house, which were not geopathic stress lines, but she could not find any other explanation. As soon as I dowsed, I agreed there was a definite negative Earth energy present, but not familiar to me either.

While investigating it over a few weeks, I dowsed for inspiration about understanding and handling this new intrusion. The technique I had adopted for dealing with geopathic stress did not affect it. I was also concerned to discover that it seemed even more potent than typical geopathic stress. Desperate for insights into the nature of the problem, I named it Earth Fatigue as a working title. The term had come into my mind as a 'clair' definition, creating an identity and making it easier to focus on a solution. Eventually, I found a highly modified version of my geopathic stress treatment that solved Debbie's problem. I also felt that referencing it by the term Earth Fatigue showed an understanding of the real issue and helped me focus on developing a remedy.

I detected Earth Fatigue as a weakness in our Earth's own planetary energy system. I have already said that for the planet to have such a mechanism is consistent with a universe developed by the sources and resources of Intelligent Energies. As we have all grown out of the Earth, we and the planet are inextricably related. We share a common ancestry and, like any family, maintain our links to our birth source. In this case, the links to the planet's energies help keep us well via our body energies.

At present, the Earth is suffering more than ever. It is sick, and its energies are struggling to cope, hence the name Earth Fatigue. I believe the underlying cause is planetary negativity brought on by environmental damage and negative energies from the many world traumas affecting humans, animals, plants and trees. The consequences have impacts on us because we rely on the Earth's wellbeing for us to prosper. Earth Fatigue has weakened the planet's positive influence and, like geopathic stress, harms our body energies.

The detail in these explanations came to me from the same source, which cooperates and supports all my energy work. This time the source was leading me towards a different Earth energy treatment whilst harnessing methods like those which had been proven to deal with geopathic stress. There was now a new relief process which brought that small but significant area in South Africa back into a state of wellbeing as soon as my treatment was applied.

Full indications of the damage caused by Earth Fatigue and the value of dealing with it were both confirmed when Debbie later reported the stress lines were no longer there. She told me about the mango and litchi trees which grew close to the former stress lines. She said they had not fruited for four to five years but, following my treatment, were all suddenly thriving, 'much to the delight of the monkeys.' Later, Debbie moved from the house and land but reported those trees continued to fruit, and even more trees on the site showed the same gains. It reminds us that the Earth is suffering, weakened from all manner of damage at the energy level over the centuries, particularly in recent decades. The problems first reported by Debbie are happening all over the world.

Another practitioner, Jacinta Fisher, told me about similar experiences in early 2021. Jacinta is a therapist who works with a technique known as Body Talk. A gentle process that uses interactive energies to restore people's health and wellbeing. She also lives in South Africa and found remarkable changes following the clearance of geopathic stress and Earth Fatigue on her land. I want to record her feedback.

'There have been apricots, pomegranates, grapes and healthy herbs. In the beginning, no trees were bearing fruit except for the lemon trees, which love to have their feet wet. One of the most important discoveries is that the number of mosquitoes has dwindled down to 0.5%, not even 1%. We used to have tons of mosquitoes here. The neighbours have been out shopping for seeds because they noticed their gardens flourishing after the treatment.' I later slightly widened the location I was treating for Jacinta, who afterwards reported, 'I slept well after that, and I did not have any further heart palpitations.'

I make no claims that my clearances will have that effect at every location, but any matters caused or worsened by Earth Fatigue or geopathic stress will benefit from my clearances. Her feedback and her neighbours' reactions show that dealing with the Earth energies was a triumph for Intelligent Energies. It demonstrated again what an amazing aspect of the universe these powers are.

Earth Fatigue is possibly known only to me and to those clients with whom I have discussed it, but the effects of geopathic stress have been evident for much longer. Early in my encounters with it, I learned how a number of people on different floors of a small block of flats in Dubrovnik had developed cancer. This caused the authorities to regard the block as unfit for habitation; they demolished it, turning the site into a grassed area. The example set by Dubrovnik argues for an enlightened attitude and strong determination to protect residents everywhere.

Let me repeat that because the distorted energy reduces our body's ability to keep itself well, the effects on any individual will also depend on what else our energies are coping with. As well as ageing, issues such as poor diet, low exercise, and habits such as smoking will already make it difficult for our immune system and body energies to cope. Adding geopathic stress or Earth Fatigue as a further impediment to health is more severe for those already struggling with fitness and wellbeing. Such variations help make geopathic stress inconsistent and difficult to recognise, which also helps to keep it largely unknown.

Although its presence is not easy to identify, some classic indicators show someone may be suffering from the impact of geopathic stress. They are the common and innocent symptoms I mentioned earlier, of which we should all try to be aware. They include:

- poor sleeping patterns
- waking to feel you have not had a proper night's sleep
- grinding your teeth during the night

- low energy levels
- sleepwalking
- unexplained headaches and muscle pains
- displays of severe impatience and even anger
- babies moving about their cot, pressing themselves against the bars
- grey pallor, an unwashed appearance and lifeless hair

These indicators can sometimes be severe, but not everyone affected by geopathic stress will show any apparent signs. This does not diminish its significance or the harm it brings by causing or worsening health conditions. There are reasons why there are variations in how individuals react to this genuine danger. Some are more sensitive to it, and even if they live in the same house, not everyone is necessarily equally exposed to it. For example, people lying side-by-side in bed may find one side is worse than the other according to where the stress line is situated. Nevertheless, the levels can grow over time for anyone, and no one is truly safe if they live under its influence. Here are some points to consider:

- It is not an illness but more an intolerance to potentially toxic energy.
- Some individuals seem to tolerate it naturally better than others
- Those with weaker constitutions or underlying issues are likely to suffer the most, especially the elderly
- Some will be exposed at work as an added source, while some will be free of it when they are absent and, therefore, perhaps able to find

a little relief

- It is likely that the way Covid affects us all differently is connected to how someone with geopathic stress struggles more as the virus strengthens its influence on us

Any negative energies can attach to existing or potential health threats through those areas of our physiology in which our body energies are already depleted. I first noticed this whilst sitting at the computer. A toothache began developing, yet the symptoms disappeared once I moved away. Over a couple of weeks, the pain started to appear sooner in my computer sessions, and after I had finished took longer to fade. My dentist told me she had never heard of a computer causing toothache, but that root canal treatment was indicated. The point here is that long before the pain was obvious enough to book a dental appointment, the computer's magnetic field had begun troubling me. It hurt in the exact area where my body energies were trying to combat the root decay.

Once the tooth was repaired, the energies in that part of my body returned to normal, and I could deal comfortably with the computer field again. This strongly underlines how any health condition will be made worse by intrusive energies, whether geopathic stress, Earth Fatigue, or electromagnetic fields (EMFs) such as those emanating from computers. These and similar devices are a growing concern for many who have long warned of the potential dangers of mobile/cell phones, especially for those who use them excessively. The more we allow adverse energies from electronic devices to build up in our systems, the more likely we are to suffer health problems.

As long as we remain unaware of how these electro-fields can adversely affect us, we cannot acknowledge the full consequences of their intrusions. One day, discordant Earth energies and electromagnetic fields will be perceived as a danger akin to smoking and other harmful practices. Most of us - including children - are exposed to them almost constantly and usually unwittingly. It is entirely feasible for electricity and electromagnetic fields to cause reactions through our body energy fields. Electricity is a hazardous commodity that can kill if we get too close to it. We keep it insulated to make it safer to be near, but we must still keep our distance. However, our body energies extend beyond our physical bodies to reach into electrical fields around us in our houses and other places. Interaction between our body energies and electrical fields could easily affect us with damaging consequences.

It is another issue science should be exploring for everyone's sake. The risk of such energy pollution is growing as the world's population increasingly relies on devices served by wi-fi masts and other infrastructure. How long must we wait before these failures and inaction by the authorities join the list of similar errors of judgements made in the past? For example, how soon before medical research begins examining geopathic stress as a significant factor in cancer clusters in certain, very specific locations? Little wonder many people believe governments know what is happening, but dare not make it known because they do not have the answers. Most of my work now deals with geopathic stress and Earth Fatigue. This does not include EMFs but does remove something like 70% of the problems caused by adverse energies. Eliminating geopathic stress and Earth Fatigue anywhere and everywhere would reduce our overall exposure to incompatible energy levels, leaving body energies better placed to cope with EMFs. A massive improvement on what is happening right now.

The modern world has a better grasp on many factors unknown or misunderstood in the past. In most cases, this is to our advantage. Still, sometimes we lose sight of knowledge better understood long ago when our ancestors led more natural lives and maintained a steady focus on their surroundings. They would have had adverse energies from within the Earth firmly in their sights, which might have generated fears of mythical proportions such as Medusa, Erinyes, and Hecate. A fitting, if not quite literal, acknowledgement of the incompatible and harmful influences affecting us today.

CATCHING UP WITH EINSTEIN'S PIPER

'We all dance to a mysterious tune intoned in the distance by an invisible piper.'

ALBERT EINSTEIN

Halfway through my book is a good moment to repeat its introduction as a book to enable everyone to build their own sense of reality on firmer foundations. To examine a thread which runs throughout existence, a timely opportunity to return to Einstein's perceptive and poetic quote acknowledging the presence of those positive cosmic powers which constantly affect us all. How he beautifully and eloquently sums up the nature of the universe to point science back towards spirituality and mysticism. Despite his mathematical genius, the simplicity of this imagery points us to a greater appreciation of the workings of the universe. It reaches into the soul, defining life as it is in our world of energies. To experience the full impact of Einstein's words, we only need to relate the piper directly to Intelligent Energies for the deeply meaningful truths many are yet to accept.

Far more than anyone knew at the time, Einstein was decades ahead of his counterparts. Part of the richness of his 'piper' observation is how it brings together everything at all levels of the universe: from the majesty of the galaxies to the day-to-day life of the insect, from an apple falling from the tree to the planets in orbit around our sun. We live in a solar system which grows our food and is explored by the finest minds on our planet. Some measure and understand its physicality, others sense its spirituality, and many use its energies directly and interactively. Across the world, people are now looking for new ways to establish a belief system for themselves - one which is more spiritual than secular. No doubt the planet needs a fresh outlook - however we define and apply it. Religion, mysticism, energy work, love, peace, meditation, visualisation, mindfulness, and close connections to nature all relate to a higher reality.

There is a belief the crisis of the world pandemic coronavirus since the start of 2020 was meant as a wake up call for us to change our ways. To become closer to the nature of the planet and its interactive energies, as philosophical interpretations and as our response to the Earth's cry for help. The lessons for us to address are those negative influences damaging the environment, life and social relations. The damage, in turn, generates its own negative energy imprints that spiral across the planet. They begin as individual practical events or actions, but escalate across our culture with ever-growing impacts at the energy level. Ignoring the warnings risks further consequences if we fail to remedy humankind's negative onslaught.

We can only speculate about Covid's appearance and how it might have been prompted. Energy workers know how negative energy imprints do build up and spread as part of existence. Adverse influences can interact with other negative forces to escalate damaging consequences both for Earth energies and our body energies. Forcing the planet to be less able to sustain us fully, and therefore we do not benefit from our Earth as nature intends. We see the consequences around us, but we do not recognise the full pattern.

There is a related principle to how both positive and negative energy interactions generate, known as the Laws of Attraction, and set out in the book *'Ask and It Is Given'* by Esther and Gerry Hicks. The Laws of Attraction codify aspects of positive interactions we can access directly. Properly used, they can help bring beneficial results. Esther and Gerry Hicks explain a conscious and deliberate process available to us to improve our lives and meet our needs. Our energy vibrations naturally seek out and connect like with like. The Laws of Attraction define this as 'whatever you are giving your attention to causes you to emit a vibration which equals your point of attraction.' If your point of attraction is a positive vibration, it will attract positive energies and positive consequences. The corollary is that any negative point of attention will bring negative energies and, therefore, negative outcomes.

This would also easily apply to our living planet. It has been giving attention to its needs, and the Laws of Attraction will recognise that. Intelligent Energies would have the interactive power to respond to the state of the Earth. They are capable of addressing the threats we are posing by bringing the virus upon us as a manifestation which we might recognise as a warning. They can do this by directly modifying - mutating - viruses or by prompting actions on the part of humans or animals that act as triggers. This is not to say we are being punished. The Earth is giving attention to its needs and is receiving a reaction. Tashfeen, one of my clients, emailed me at the height of Covid, observing how 'the whole world is going through some difficult times currently. However, at the same time, I believe the planet Earth is getting some time to heal itself.'

Intelligent Energies could indeed be responding through the planet's point of attraction. Its needs are being met through a virus giving it time to heal whilst alerting those able to interpret the vibrations to the need to act. Those who understand this message must take the lead in encouraging humankind to save its home. We who have understood the vibrations now have a duty to make the consequences known to everyone. Dowsing tells me this is what has been happening. The planet must be saved, and we all have the responsibility to make changes to help Intelligent Energies restore the environment. We must also recognise that cosmic energies are not specifically committed to saving humanity. They are structured to evolve and assist all life.

Many will doubt these energy connections are present, but they are a logical extension of evident cosmic forces. Scientific and other circles are speaking with increasing urgency about the limited time available to make enough changes to ensure a viable planet for future generations. The scientific assessment is based only on scientists' perceived knowledge of the physics of the planet as it struggles to survive. No general consideration is yet given to damage from other interactive and damaging energy fields with which we must also contend. Industry, pesticides, waste, deforestation, interference and losses to wildlife arise from harmful modern practices. They increase the energy burden for the planet, and we bear the consequences both directly and as geopathic stress and Earth Fatigue. There is, however, another side to that coin. Without knowledge of the harm caused by adverse energies, scientists, the media, and others are equally unaware of the potential help to redress the damage through positive interactive energies. My processes for dealing with geopathic stress and Earth Fatigue prove changes are possible, as do the principles central to those organisations committed to spreading connectedness.

Yes, there has been a relentless downward spiral, we all know that, but there are also upward spirals in play. There are, therefore, two reasons why Intelligent Energies and related interactions must be understood. Firstly, to help limit or prevent our further negative impacts on people and the planet. Secondly, to use the world of energies for positive gains. This is not just about the changes the interactive energies can make to the physical environment directly; it is also about the new ideas it can inspire to help us better manage our problems.

The Covid pandemic began huge personal, national, and international alarm, hardship, and grief; there's no denying the dark and challenging experiences endured by so many. However, we also experienced positives: communities coming together, people helping one another, especially to aid the weak and vulnerable. Less pollution quickly showed a better world during the first pandemic wave, including for people in Northern India seeing the Himalayas 100 miles away for the first time in decades. A sense of peace and quiet arose from local townscapes, more relaxed than usual. Yes, there was fear and inconvenience, but also a sense of sharing, of cross-planetary fund-raising for great causes, and emotional outbursts of thanks to the health and other front-line workers having to go far beyond their duties. Good humour, solidarity, new ways of working and a glimpse of how life might be with a different approach all encouraged an improved perspective. Desirable in its own right, but also for producing positive energy imprints, helping to create better vibes for the planet and ourselves.

Rising awareness of environmental change and care for the environment is not only critical to the planet's survival but might also forge a stronger connection between us and the real nature of the world we inhabit. Intelligent Energies, aligned with James Lovelock's Gaia theory, also connect with a third famous concept: The Findhorn Foundation based in Kinross, Scotland. Findhorn has been around since 1962 and will repay everyone's attention. It has actively practised a philosophy which completely matches energy workers' experiences and perspectives.

Findhorn publicity quotes how founders Eileen and Peter Caddy and Dorothy Maclean 'supplemented their diet by growing their own food.' And continues 'the inner source of wisdom they contacted daily included the intelligence of nature, and when they listened to and applied the wisdom they received, the garden flourished. As they progressed in their practice of attuning to the intelligence of nature, they came to understand they were actually engaged in a process of co-creation with nature.' The founders' working philosophy was clear and translated into direct results which readily reflect the influence of Intelligent Energies in which:

> All living things have a working energy system.
>
> Everything inorganic also has its own version of an energy field
>
> The entire cosmos has its own subatomic interactive energy field or fields
>
> All energy fields interact with each other and with the cosmic field
>
> The cosmic field does so with awareness and intelligence
>
> Everything that happens has an energy imprint
>
> Interactions can correct negative energies to bring positive change.

Adopt those principles, and everything is fully explained. They offer answers and solutions, but nothing is fully explained when we leave them out. We can use the principles to understand ancient knowledge and beliefs whilst also using them to encourage us to look to a new future as an advanced civilisation. Einstein's metaphor of a distant piper works well alongside the theme of Intelligent Energies to explain the order behind life and the universe. We can read the same theme into the labels offered by different cultures and perspectives. Though they may frame them differently, many ancient beliefs share similar principles. Over time these ideas have lost their impact as they became increasingly out of step with modern thinking.

With its ever-growing free will and independent

thought, intelligent human life has flooded our planet. The instincts, insights and experiences of the ancients who lived less frenetically, more in tune with nature and untroubled by endless streams of information have been overwhelmed. Einstein's piper is now having a hard time being heard; even so, the tune goes on. Universal laws apply regardless of who is listening - although they do work best for those consciously at one with them.

There are encouraging signs upon which new thinking can be built for future generations. Better informed and more environmentally friendly farming techniques are spreading. They are good for the farming industry and for the planet. Former Formula One racing champion Jody Scheckter runs Laverstoke Park Farm in Hampshire, England. It is an organic, biodynamic enterprise combining livestock and arable farming. He connects the latest techniques with a determination to work with nature by replicating how things have been done for thousands of years. He believes those who force their land through pesticides and other unnatural measures are killing the cycle of nature. His approach is so beneficial and successful that he now works with elite athletes who want the best in healthy, nutritious food. Customers have found they no longer need to use supplements to top up what modern food often leaves out of their diets.

Biodynamics is also spreading across farming and being applied to vineyards and wine. The difference is being widely seen to be a much higher quality product. What is surprising about biodynamics is that the methodology also depends on the lunar calendar and carrying out tasks in appropriate sequences and timing. Some growers also often introduce the Zodiac into their growing cycles. There is an added belief that combining traditional farming as a holistic mix of dairy, vegetables, grains, chickens etc., together on one farm brings more benefits.

All yield better quality produce by respecting the wisdom of past practices and taking a fresh approach for the twenty-first century. There has to be a reason for such successful advances - once again, cosmic Intelligent Energies fit the pattern.

LAW AND ORDER IN THE UNIVERSE

'There is no logical way to the discovery of these elemental laws. There is only the way of intuition, which is helped by a feeling for the order lying behind the appearance.'

ALBERT EINSTEIN

Einstein's observation further reinforces the case for an organised structure behind the universe instead of chance and coincidences. His sense of intuition and the 'order lying behind the appearance' is revealed, reverberating through the world of energies. The ordered nature of the universe is not disputed. How that order developed has become the mystery which separates our standard perspectives. Chance and coincidence hardly amount to a reasoned source - they only define an outcome as an effect without a cause. Following this weak scientific perspective, we are meant to believe a cosmos of staggering complexities, most of which we do not comprehend, just materialised along with other complexities we have not yet dreamed of. Mainstream scientific confidence remains unabated in believing that life and the universe were fabricated precisely as needed but instigated by chance. That is not an explanation; it is an admission that science has no explanation. It should be the starting point for greater enlightenment, a driving force to find what does lie behind the appearance. Most of all, it should inspire a desire to learn more from events which science cannot yet understand.

The present elemental laws of science partly explain the known physics of the universe. It seems Einstein was suggesting 'unscientific' intuition could lie behind some of science's most significant discoveries. In this regard, I have shown an inspirational process through Intelligent Energies is available for every discovery ever made by anyone, regardless of their qualifications. A process to prompt achievements in the arts and science and generate instincts which allow a person or an animal to take beneficial action beyond conscious thought. Lives are constantly in tune with Intelligent Energies, consciously or subconsciously. From the Laws of Attraction, the phrase 'giving your attention to' means nothing must articulate its needs to get the help it requires. Attention to whatever is required is paid simply by having that requirement, not by stating it.

This is a vital property whenever words are impossible for plant and animal life to form, but their needs are nevertheless present. Any state of being is known by and accessible to Intelligent Energies. Needs apply equally, whether or not they can be articulated or understood consciously. This also extends to all the ingredients which first needed to be gathered in the right and exceedingly complex way to develop the physical universe. Even when there is no personal, spoken contact between them, the energies within all matter in all its stages are always an integral part of the entire universe. Once again, the energies within atoms connect through vibrations, their point of attraction.

The energy imprint of any 'need' is enough to build

a vital link with the Intelligent Energies. To 'ask and be given' is the path for everything to evolve and develop according to their needs and opportunities. Energy combinations explain the events guiding the subsequent progression of an interactive cosmos up to and from the Big Bang. There is nothing to say this development process has reached its highest state - the ultimate universe may still be billions of years away.[4]

For sentient beings, there is inevitably a more direct association with the energies as we spell out our needs, consciously or subconsciously. So many creative advances made by individuals confirm what is possible at the personal level and on the grand cosmic scale. Because they can happen subconsciously, seemingly inadvertent personal connections are plentiful, though not always easy to recognise for the interventions they are. Those inspirations which strike people in creative fields were once described in Amanda McBroom's

---

[4] In August 2019, *New Scientist* magazine referred to theories that the universe may not have begun with a 'Big Bang', but once created, it collapsed itself every many billion years before starting again as another universe. This is reminiscent of Lee Smolin's concept of 'Daughter Universes.' It is important to note that, yet again, the process orchestrating the life, death and resurrection of a new universe (with all the data learned from previous ones to guide the new one) is likely to be that of Intelligent Energies. It is also a principle which relates to the seasonal new and re-growth we find in the plant world and even mirrors the process of reincarnation found in many religions and beliefs. Many people regard this as part of our life pattern, our energy systems repeatedly appearing and reappearing as different lifetimes, each time learning new lessons. [The Big Bang theory is no longer popular, and all my references to the cosmic role of Intelligent Energies apply to universes re-growing by any scientific principle. Intelligent Energies are the most likely mechanism to account for all death and re-growth, and I continue to use the Bang as an allegory for whatever science finally decides .l.l]

account of how she came to write her song 'The Rose'. The song became a massive success after it was used as the title song for the film of the same name. According to Amanda's website, it began as she was driving along listening to a song on the radio. Much as she admired the lyric, she did not agree with its sentiment, prompting the thought: 'What is love'? She continues: 'suddenly, it was as if someone had opened a window in the top of my head. Words came pouring in. I had to keep reciting them to myself as I drove faster and faster towards home so I wouldn't forget them.' She arrived home and rushed to the piano; within 10 minutes, her classic song was completed.

The idea of insights 'coming through a window in the head' has been used by others as a metaphor for inspiration. It raises so much we can find for ourselves at the heart of interactive Intelligent Energies. Or, to put it another way, at the heart of working with the universe. Not everyone will find a 'pot of gold' or a hit song, but we can find genuine help and support whenever we open ourselves up to those energies.

Energy workers, therapists, practitioners, and others have different functions, interpretations, and labels for what they do, but all depend on the interactions of energies. Feng Shui, healing, dowsing, reflexology, mindfulness, and yoga are just some examples. If we fully embrace this perspective, we can explore a new world. We can raise awareness around the validity of the many events, happenings and experiences presently defying those bound by a scientific framework. A framework which has become centuries out of date.

We can share a glimpse of a new order through the

energy healing technique. As an illustration, a client once asked for help to deal with pain from an injured thumb. She had no idea what she had done, but I gave her some contact healing, improving things for a few days. When she got in touch again, we agreed to try absent healing. As well as being more convenient, absent healing is valuable because remote energy precisely targets the body energy source of the pain. [Another amazing property of healing]. My client later rang to say that before sending her off to sleep, the healing produced vibrations in the joint of her thumb, the base of her first finger, her wrist, and her shoulder. She also reported the remote healing had eased the pain again.

This revealed how the healing energy had been attracted to four locations, even though she had only felt pain in her thumb. From this, we concluded her problem had probably been caused by a fall she had not noticed during one of her jujitsu lessons. This had not been evident earlier and shows how the system with which healers work offers the potential to contribute to many more patient health issues as part of the health service infrastructure.

We should not be afraid to challenge modern science. Early scientists directed standing stones as part of their culture and had brilliant minds. They displayed astonishing mathematical, astronomical and engineering abilities and showed sensitivity and spirituality. These multifaceted aspects of their personalities motivated them to design and construct extraordinary monuments now discovered throughout the world. In doing so, they came far closer to nature, the changing seasons, and the real cosmos than their descendants have managed to do. There is much they could teach us.

Our ancestors held beliefs based on interactions with nature long before later societies moved on to more recognisable spiritual and religious beliefs. They knew what orthodoxy has forgotten, but those of us who practise from outside science continue to prove a dimension missing from what is usually represented as the rational view of our world. We hold a more unified understanding of the universe and a better sense of that 'order lying behind the appearance.' Our experiences add to the laws determined by science and to the order which has been created.

We are approaching a time when a much more unified view of reality will become more acceptable to a wider range of people. There is hope for greater enlightenment than ever before. Those threads of energy which run through the whole of existence, with their power to interact, have brought balance to the universe. They initiated the laws science has fathomed, and those it has not. Subatomic theories continue to change the way we look at the universe. Eventually, there will be a time for adding new elemental laws to explain so much more.

NATURE'S WAYS

'We still do not know one thousandth of one percent of what nature has revealed to us.'

ALBERT EINSTEIN

Einstein's point that we do not fully understand true nature was no doubt aimed at explaining the depth, variety, and ingenuity of that part of the natural world which has - or had - been revealed. Since his time, much more has been learned, but, for the most part, that greater knowledge raises further difficult questions about how nature operates. Wherever scientists address their topics, no account of the role or the practical implications of interactive energies can be taken. We need to rethink our definition of nature.

Nature is commonly interpreted as a reference to all aspects of all organic life forms on Earth, from plants and microbes to humans. The faculty of body energies and the sophistication of DNA have always been a part of what nature teaches us. Natural forces consciously and directly cooperate with every being to guide, harmonise, evolve and heal. For those tuned in, it is possible to feel surrounded by - and a part of - these energy fields. With experience, we can establish a robust and immersive connection for ourselves. I sense it as the difference between seeing the trees of the forest and *being with* the trees of the forest. Not unlike the notion of mindfulness, it is an emotional and satisfying attunement for us which brings us physically closer to our place in nature.

The forces which cross the universe to interact with organic life are the same forces which activated and influenced the laws of physics. They are a part of nature and part of the physical cosmos. That, too, must be regarded as natural and helps re-positions how we see nature. In years gone by, Nature Study was a single subject taught in UK schools, but long since overtaken by the fields of biology and botany, physics, chemistry, and now newer sciences. The more we look at the universe in all its detail, the more we rely on science and its latest discoveries in different fields to make sense of the arrangements up close. However, reaching for more distinct disciplines is symptomatic of how we need to catch up on the bigger interactive and cohesive picture.

Science prides itself on the rigour with which it examines all ideas, especially those which break new ground. New findings or proposals are subject to peer review by other scientists, and changes in standard thinking are only accepted through the consensus of the appropriate scientific communities. For the most part, this is an understandable attempt to ensure scientists are working from the same base. It allows minimal disruption from any thinking that might threaten scientific approval's integrity.

There may be no quarrel with that, but the consequences for science go beyond due diligence. The same scientific integrity often leads to unjust rejection or even to professional ridicule when new thinking is too much for some to accept. To non-scientists, the profession seems overprotective of a regime already proven to delay scientific advances for decades. Perhaps even blocking them permanently if those with new knowledge remain thwarted or lose their passion. German philosopher Arthur Schopenhauer once said, 'All truth passes through three stages. First, it is ridiculed. Second, it is violently opposed. Third, it is accepted as being self-evident.' He died in 1860, but his words are as relevant today as they were in his time.

When we look back at what we believed to be true - but has since been proven otherwise - it is often hard to know why it took us years to see the obvious. An item on the BBC News website, 4 October 2016, carried a piece about the horrors of scurvy. The deadly condition caused misery and death to sailors in the eighteenth century. The piece recorded how 'The disease during long sea voyages was often more dangerous than enemy action. One British expedition to raid Spanish holdings in the Pacific Ocean in the 1740s lost 1300 of an original complement of 2000 men to the illness. The symptoms were horrendous and the risks huge, but we know now that the killer disease resulted from no more than a lack of Vitamin C.' This simple fact not only confirms the solution, it also reinforces nature's interactions as the fundamental source of health and wellbeing. We vitally need vitamin C, and nature provides it in citrus fruit.

Scurvy had long been recognised as a persistent and often fatal condition, yet there were already suggestions that citrus fruit could be an effective remedy. Centuries ago, explorer Sir Richard Hawkins was advocating lemons as a solution. Over a hundred years later, in 1747, James Lind, surgeon aboard the HMS Salisbury, was able to trial the remedies recommended in previous years, which included administering citrus fruits. The trials effectively proved vitamin C as a prevention and cure, but even though beneficial results for other ailments were generally known to abound in nature, nothing hastened the authorities to act.

Delays by science, the government, and the Admiralty collectively or individually led to a failure to apply answers during the intervening years from 1622. Ultimately, they all had to thank the perseverance of a single ship's doctor, who was determined to find the way forward for himself. It took another 50 years before the Admiralty took James Lind's work on board. They finally ordered lemon juice rations for all naval personnel in 1795. The lessons of that debacle can teach us a great deal.

Despite modern structures and communications - including a robust investigative press and media - such ignorance and delay can and still does happen. In their own context, many similar obstructions today block progress and free thinking. Just as in Lind's case, those with many decades of experience in fields going back centuries find resistance to their abilities and contributions. Barriers still exist, built by a lack of knowledge and an absence of serious inquiry by those who should be leading the quest for advancement.

The implications of living within an interactive cosmic force of nature offer a breathtaking potential for benefits to us all. If we accept this and work with it, we could gain from practical and cultural changes across society. Instead, those with the most power and responsibility often dismiss the facts, whilst louder voices drown out others who wish to tell a different story. Aeronautical pioneer Orville Wright reminds us: 'If we all worked on the assumption that what is accepted as true is really true, there would be little hope of advance.'

Professor of Science Rupert Sheldrake writes on a similar understanding to my own, and in a private exchange, he generously called my work important. He refers to his topic as Morphic Resonance and Morphic Fields. The Professor's approach to the theme is that there are fields which influence plant and animal behaviour to set up patterns to account for their evolution and growth. The concept of Intelligent Energies sits well with Morphic Resonance/Fields, though I go further by showing how the same sentient energies influence the entire cosmos and all its rules. The interactions do not only apply to living organisms.

Pressure will have to grow from outside the scientific community in using all modern channels to focus minds on the weaknesses of the standard scientific outlook. That is the flawed blueprint that cannot fully account for the complexities of life, the universe, or the daily successes of energy workers.

The scientific platform still fails to recognise how geopathic stress affects us and how it can be identified and cleared. My website links to a DVD about geopathic stress and shows cows in a shed refusing to enter a stall which had tested as geopathically stressed. All the cows walked straight past it. Clearly, at some level, they were aware of the potential risk from the negative force of nature within. They avoid the ground, which carries evidence currently beyond scientific comprehension. Yet, ironically, scientists were credited with helping establish the influence of geopathic stress many years ago.

In the Journal of Action for ME, dowser Alf Riggs records fascinating details about the historical, technical understanding of geopathic stress. In 1922, doctors in Germany worked with dowsers to satisfy themselves about how certain Earth rays were responsible for many serious health conditions. In 1929, dowser Gustav von Pohl was officially invited to check properties throughout the Bavarian town of Vilsbiburg. His findings alerted the authorities to many properties he regarded as being geopathically stressed and which he thought would likely have led to cancers. The results were then confirmed by the town's medical chiefs, whose records showed forty-two stressed houses had been affected by up to seven cancer deaths during the period under review.

In Stettin, Poland, the city medical officer Dr Hager reviewed more than 5000 cases in which he, too, established influences by electromagnetic fields. Dr Hartmann, who discovered the part of Earth's natural magnetic system now known as the Hartmann Grid, produced a significant report confirming how disease was another feature of underground disturbance, with the matter of location again coming into account. It is a straightforward premise that body energies, unable to do their job properly, lead to an interference with health.

More research might establish whether this could be responsible for cases of catastrophic failure of body systems. It could easily be a critical factor in degenerative conditions such as Parkinson's Disease or

Motor Neurone Disease. This is not yet proven, but nor should it be ruled out. Those affected, now or in the future, deserve the critical topic of intrusions into body energies to be addressed to measure their impact and find potential new ways to help.

The scientific findings concerning adverse energies from the 1920s to the 1980s have never been disproved, but neither have they been pursued enthusiastically. As a result, adverse Earth energies remain under the radar for most people. We still face the shocking tragedy of doctors unwittingly sending patients home to geopathically stressed homes which continue to contribute adversely to their health issues. Moreover, a proportion of their patients will lie in stressed hospital beds where their health conditions are at risk, and treatment is slowed. Too many elderly in care homes will suffer the same way, no matter how professionally well-treated they are. Nowhere is immune from geopathic stress or Earth Fatigue.

Since geopathic stress is driven by naturally occurring but distorted fields, I long ago started to consider a critical question I am still often asked. How can my process to clear underground geopathic stress permanently and from a distance work as a practical solution? It is impossible to change or eliminate any of its geological or similar sources. The subsurface features which generate geopathic stress remain, so it must continue to be created. My intervention as an energy worker is, by definition, an energy solution. It uses nature in the broader sense of interactive energies to restore the distorted Earth energy to its natural, harmless state. My remote interactive process does this as soon as I have applied it. From that point, the energy distortion is reversed as it is being created. In a nanosecond, the geopathic stress develops and is made safe again. The distorted rays do not get beyond that creation point and no longer reach the Earth's surface. The naturally formed geopathic stress immediately disappears just as naturally through the energy cycle I establish for each location I treat.

The treatment is not the work of the universal energies alone. If it were, human involvement would not be required. As with remote healing and dowsing, nothing occurs until communication and interaction with the cosmic energies are established. My body energies link to Intelligent Energies to initiate their connection to the energies of geopathic stress and Earth Fatigue. Only when this rapport is established can the details of my techniques come into play.

All of which reinforces the status of the world experienced outside science but within the field of energy work. Topics and even mysteries that puzzle scientists are often easily explained through understanding the sentient forces crossing the cosmos. One such incident turned up in a trailer for a British television programme, 'Naked and Marooned', in which adventurer Ed Stafford was left to fend for himself for two months using only his survival skills. In an interview, he mentioned how, whilst making the programme, he had been greatly helped by the advice of Aborigines he had met before starting his venture. They taught him how their ancestors have long known that relying on what we would see as our conscious brain will cause real problems in the isolation they face during 'walkabout' in Australia's outback. They were aware of a sense of overload, the opposite of the immersive connectedness to nature they were seeking. Nature taught them we have three brains: one in the stomach, one in the heart, and the one in our head, enabling them to deal with the impact on their senses in an extraordinary way. By sitting in a circle of stones, they can restore mental balance. This ancient advice was passed to Stafford, who used the technique and reported on how it had worked successfully for him, and that he was happy to recommend it.

Safe science will struggle to take this on board as a cause-and-effect process, but through the influence of Intelligent Energies and healing techniques, a combination of body energies and cosmic forces explain the inexplicable. An Aboriginal energy healing takes place through the forces of nature transferred by stone circles. There is an apparent link between the stones used by that culture and the larger standing stones found worldwide. Science recognises the mathematical and astronomical significance of the stone circles but cannot fully show how and why they were erected in construction projects requiring monumental efforts by those responsible. If a small circle of stones helps the mental equilibrium of those sitting at the centre of them, what might be the power of Stonehenge and its equivalents worldwide? What powers and abilities did they confer or assist, and what is the full significance of the alignments? Is it only to mark the changing seasons, or are the stones connecting humankind to another aspect of Intelligent Energies? In a similar vein, what exactly are the powers of pyramids?

With its personal and universal energies, nature is incredibly influential. There is no part of the scientific model to allow for the calming effects of rings of stones or, as another example, crystal therapy. We are not accustomed to thinking of the body working and interacting directly with nature. Nonetheless, our body energies are part of the human organism, connecting every part of us to a worldwide and universal source of incoming power and information. Through interactive energies, nature helps us attune to what we face at any time. It has the means to help us, whether through therapies, healing plants, or other techniques such as monoliths.

Television scientist Michael Mosley experimented on himself to demonstrate we do indeed have, in his words, 'a brain in our gut.' By swallowing a miniature camera, he could trace how the stomach's work in digesting food was aided by neurons, 'as many as in a cat's head.' A significant finding in line with ancient Aboriginal knowledge. The neurons do not operate as a conscious thought process but ensure the stomach is better able to do its job in a particularly coordinated and sophisticated way. It allows us to digest food and utilise essential vitamins while maintaining contact with the head brain. We are all aware of a related dimension to this through those emotions in which our heads and stomachs jointly react when we experience fear, stress, excitement, or that strong sense of welcome relief. We get 'butterflies' in our stomachs because we are nervous or may feel sick or lose our appetites in times of crisis. This extra brain power chimes with the Intelligent Energy signals passed to me by my gut, which I described earlier.

The three brains of the head, heart and stomach, and the connection with stones in a circle, have been a part of Aboriginal understanding for thousands of years, yet only recently has science acknowledged any link. As Einstein says, there is so much nature can teach us - including lessons from ancient culture and modern energy work.

The practical implication of the successful calming contribution of rings of stone is that the physiological connection must be at the energy level. There is no other route by which they can affect us. For now, it marks another point where life experiences clash with scientific boundaries. Energy work demonstrates how interactive energies are natural - and constantly affect daily life for everyone. This includes when sitting in a stone circle.

There are many ramifications to be addressed once we begin to accept energy intelligence throughout nature. Some are more practical than others. Geopathic stress and Earth Fatigue are significant concerns because discordant energies can greatly influence us. To make matters worse, this impact is set to spread. In practice, it can be found almost everywhere. Mine workings close to our home, where we first discovered geopathic stress, are just one well-known source for creating or increasing the rates of underground streams. Subterranean fissures, rocks, tunnelling, extraction, constructions, and even roadworks are also considered triggers. The potency varies according to the strength of the source, which can change from time to time - mainly when heavy rainfall affects underground watercourses.

One new concern is fracking, an intensively invasive disturbance to the Earth and possibly set to expand and create consequences not yet recognised. Therefore, we must take geopathic stress seriously and then accept the intrusive practice of fracking as a new source of its adverse influence on our health. There is already much controversy around the environmental and social impacts of blasting the planet to recover shale gas. Dowsing shows me it is a practice that does and will continue to trigger more geopathic stress and bad health for millions worldwide.

The energy consequences of fracking must be thoroughly investigated to confirm the risks involved. There is a considerable danger that we are lost in the sort of closed thinking which in the past has led to widespread exposure to such dangers as DDT, asbestos, lead pipes and smoking, as well as the assumption that it was safe for military personnel to be present during atomic bomb tests. The modern threat is not being fully addressed by those with close connections to the fracking controversy, such as the industry, Government planners, or even protesters. Nor can it ever be addressed until we become more knowledgeable and respectful of our planet. Those who do know the dangers are the only ones who can change the thinking, which is a risk to us all.

Fracking is just one example of the problems we face when, as a culture, we rely so heavily on opinion weakened by its failure to address sympathetically issues which sceptics may find too challenging. Recognising interactive energies and the value of ancient knowledge about nature will help us all.

TESTING TIMES FOR SCIENCE

'Those who have the privilege to know have the duty to act and in that action are the seeds of new knowledge.'

ALBERT EINSTEIN

I have the privilege 'to know' how interacting energies are an active and constant part of everything in the universe. In practice, there is no aspect of existence to which they are irrelevant, including the environment, relationships, science, medicine, health, the arts, etc. Health issues are paramount to everyone, and it is not surprising how in an age of mass communication, vast numbers of the world's population are taking the opportunity to examine complementary therapies and active energies for themselves. Even so, this worldwide and positive test bed is still too readily dismissed by sceptics. Those of us who do know must take action to spread the word.

Effective testing of human experiences does not only take place in scientific experiments or environments. Those abilities demonstrated by healers, dowsers and others engaged in energy work are constantly being considered and trialled before being accepted by satisfied clients acting on their own initiative. Understandably, the public often seeks energy remedies only as a last resort; in my case, many are recommended by their friends, qualified professionals or others with direct experience. They almost always agree how remote healing, dowsing, or my clearing the geopathic stress have had the promised effect - often dramatically so.

I have been told of houses left unsold for some time but quickly selling once geopathic stress had been dealt with. Clients often write to say their partner, children or other family members have confirmed that the cleared house has become noticeably different, even to those unaware that anything had been done. The following is a typical reaction:

'Even the air feels lighter, and it somehow helped me remove some of my own clutter from the house. My family are all very badly affected by geopathic stress when exposed to it, especially my mother and sister. I actually waited until they noticed a difference in my house before I told them about you.' Beyond any question, my client's family felt a different atmosphere for themselves.

Another client reported how following a clearance, the glassware in his cabinet had an extra sparkle, while one told me how he found the sound from his hi-fi system after my clearance 'now much more natural, more like a live performance.' Nothing I had done by neutralising the adverse Earth energies could have introduced any added physical sparkle to a room or glassware, nor have technically improved sound quality. The clearances must, therefore, enable body energies to improve our senses of sight and hearing. We know geopathic stress interferes with our immune system, reducing its capacity to keep us well. For it to impair, even slightly, our vision or hearing shows how it also adversely affects all our senses. Every function and aspect of our wellbeing is potentially reduced when distorted Earth energies affect us.

Each energy worker is privileged to observe how events occur in a universe very different from the commonly accepted one. Whether or not it was Einstein's intention, his quote above supports all who struggle to be heard when ideas are too advanced for some to comprehend. If we who know have a duty to act, those who would regard themselves as informed have a responsibility to listen.

Einstein shared the drive from his 'knowing' whilst being underestimated by those he wished to inform. Like other scientists before and since, his persistence paid off, and he was eventually accepted as being amongst the greatest scientific minds of all time. He also actively promoted social, moral and artistic awareness. He acknowledged spiritual values and influences which, in his day as now, have little scientific backing. Some past and present-day scientists share some of those finer points, but Einstein's ideas are demonstrably closer to the realities of energy work than most.

If he had encountered the evidence for remote healing and dowsing at first-hand, he would almost certainly have been firmly behind the concept of Intelligent Energies as the force responsible for everything he knew, discovered, and believed. Like Darwin, all Einstein lacked was a personal awareness of the full nature of the interactive powers of energies. Two great scientific minds were hampered by lacking exposure to those natural forces. An obstacle that remains as scientific beliefs continue to clash with the direct experiences of energy workers and our clients.

Through the work of more and more energy practitioners in a growing range of different fields, a greater understanding of natural forces is beginning to emerge. Even so, most authorities making critical decisions affecting our lives remain reluctant to address this potential. There is no coordinated appraisal of what is regularly achieved by those who work with energies. Every day, individual lives are improved by treatments or practices ignored by a cultural orthodoxy which disproportionately influences public opinion.

Aside from the fact that they cannot account for the claims of energy workers and their clients, scientists remain sceptical about the work because the improvements appear only to the client and their practitioner. Each event in this worldwide test bed of energy experiences is a single case and statistically irrelevant. Millions of examples and accounts of treatments across the planet add up to a different story and a clearer perspective. Matthew Manning is said to be the most scientifically tested healer in the UK, if not the world, and has been endorsed by the UK's late Sir David Frost. In a series of medically tested events, Matthew even brought about changes to cancer cells. His website records his abilities and experiences, which mystify medical professionals. Despite his successes, there is no public evidence to show science is paying any serious attention.

The work begun by Gustav von Pohl is amongst many references to beliefs that geopathic stress might be a significant factor in cancer. So far as I am aware, there has been no robust modern research into any connection between incidents of cancer and the presence of geopathic stress. The reason for this can only be a reluctance to spend scarce research funds on a possible cause that would depend on accepting the role of body energies in health and wellbeing. If this were the case, it would become an added reason to begin urgently examining energies as a part of our physiology. Proof of their presence and influence could be achieved quickly and cheaply. It would lead to the potential for a significant breakthrough in cancer causes and treatment as well as healthcare generally. Such a prize is too valuable to ignore.

The practical problems for current medical science are easy to see. Talking with a group of hospital consultants once, I raised the topic of healing and the National Health Service. I was surprised to learn there was no opposition to my claims about healing. During the discussion, the consultants' main objection was not whether healers could heal, but the lack of structure for medical staff to bring reliable healers in to help reduce the pressures on the Health Service. This reminded me of my client with the back injury and the reaction of her consultant. But I had another case in which the same principle had far more significant implications. Soon after I began a healing session for a client suffering pain in her eye and ear; she told me she was feeling the healing energy through sensations behind her eye and not where she had the physical pain. Subsequent hospital tests proved she had a tumour behind her eye. Nobody had that information at the time of the healing session, but the healing energies went straight there and began to work on it. This puts everything about interactive energies beyond reasonable doubt. It is a compelling indicator of what might be possible if healers and medical staff could work more closely together.

Unfortunately, there is little appetite for a controlled consideration of the benefits healers could deliver, so the public is deterred from accessing the help they need. Healing experiences provide objective evidence, but without the profile and support to command attention, the value of complementary treatments across various therapies and fields remains uncoordinated. For decades, healers have been calling for a structure to feed our complementary therapies into the health profession in an organised way. We know it will take a massive commitment from all sides, demanding government input and, in turn, requiring government and professional confidence. So far, these authorities have failed in their responsibility to listen to 'those who have the privilege to know.' We must address this inertia.

For now, the damaging effects of geopathic stress on health conditions must remain tended to by practitioners unaware of adverse energies. Patients continue to suffer, bringing massive problems for authorities, nationally and internationally. Medical care is undermined by influences that staff cannot treat or identify. Alongside this, an overwhelmed health system struggles to deal with familiar and unfamiliar disorders. Modern pharmaceuticals' many harmful side effects further challenge good healthcare for patients and medical practitioners. Though powerful, drugs often create additional difficulties for the medical profession and those taking the medications.

Meanwhile, wide-ranging and successful techniques amongst energy therapies account for treatments such as Body Talk, Bowen Technique, reflexology as well as Bach flower remedies, homeopathy and more. Remedies which are controversial because they can be explained only by reference to interactive energies. Nothing highlights this more than homeopathy. The process depends upon an active mixture being repeatedly diluted until, for practical purposes, there is no recognisable trace left of the original. Paradoxically, the more the remedy is diluted, the stronger it is claimed to become. This is an impossibility for science which therefore concludes it cannot be a serious treatment. The only alternative explanation science has for any health gains following homeopathic or other energy treatments is the familiar one of the placebo effect. I mentioned this earlier, but it is well worth a closer look.

Placebos apparently achieve health benefits which are more effective than some orthodox medicines. Conventional pharmaceuticals can be licensed as treatments despite being no more than 30-35% effective. Statistically, this makes them no better than placebos but at a level of efficiency easily surpassed by healers and techniques such as homeopathy. Scientists cannot explain how the placebo effect happens, but they find it a handy counter to any energy healing success, even though the circumstances of energy treatments in no way match how a placebo trial is manipulated.

A member of the UK's Science and Technology Committee admitted that placebo trials include some degree of deception. Those receiving a placebo are told they are having medical treatment when they are not. With homeopathy and other forms of healing, the therapists make no such assurances. There is no deception; few clients convince themselves beforehand that the healing will work for them. Many energy healing treatments also induce physical sensations during their application; the placebo effect does not have this effect, so it cannot be responsible for successful energy healing.

Medical science will not satisfactorily explain placebo until it accepts it is triggered through the interactive energies they dismiss or fail to see. In fact, those patients who respond to 'fake' treatments in placebo trials may well be connecting themselves to the same active, cosmic healing forces reached by healers when helping clients. While going through a placebo trial, some participants will subconsciously align themselves with the universal healing energies and generate their own healing event. Placebo does not explain healing - but healing energies do explain placebo.

Clinical trials on homeopathic treatments do seem to contradict themselves. This could reflect more on the nature of the trials rather than the practicalities of successful homeopathy. The homeopathic principle rests on treating like with like to build up immunity. Immunisation is an accepted methodology confirmed by the UK's Science and Technology Advisory Committee. However, the members cautioned that the immunity principle was not necessarily transferable to all fields. They concluded like-for-like immunisation was too weak as a generality to support any effect of homeopathy. Nonetheless, it is how immunisation works when low doses of the cause of a condition are injected to stimulate protection and is therefore relevant. Exactly how that general principle is rationalised in current medical thinking should not be cited to dismiss what is happening at the energy level. Homeopathy and energies have their own rules.

To prescribe a treatment, homeopaths must identify the correct source of a disorder and apply what they regard as the most appropriate remedy. If the identified cause and remedy are not correctly matched, the treatment will be less effective or not effective at all. When this happens in homeopathic consultations, the potential cause and the proposed treatment will be reconsidered, and the remedy adjusted - just as it is with orthodox medications. However, if a single test fails, the trial and the principle of homeopathy are unjustly nullified. Tests of any kind can throw up contradictions, but it is hard to escape the fact that the biggest hurdle remaining is the puzzle of how a substance can be physically diluted whilst repeatedly making it more powerful. It seems impossible, but if we bring energy transfers into the reckoning, there is a perfectly reasonable explanation.

The laws of mainstream physics only recognise the dilution of the original healing ingredient each time water is added. The weakened mixture is shaken before adding more water to dilute it further. Adding more and more water continuously weakens the physical property of the original ingredient until virtually nothing is left of it. For science, whatever cure may have been present initially has now disappeared.

Homeopaths believe this purely physical weakening process is not all that is happening. They say each physical dilution of their initial preparation enhances its power because the memory of water concentrates the potency of each mixture. This brief explanation may hinder more than it helps because sceptics are not likely to believe water can have a memory and are unlikely to give it much credibility as a reasoned argument. It is not a bad summary of what could be happening through the power of energies. A simple, plausible principle is involved, though it needs a complete explanation.

For example, at the start of the homeopathic process, there may be 100cc of pure water. However, every cubic centimetre of that original water could scientifically carry the 'cellular' memory of the entire 100cc. It is scientifically accepted that the property of every single cell of an organism has all the information for the whole being through its DNA. Similarly, when a laser-created hologram is broken into tiny pieces, the unbroken original image is still available from the pieces. To some degree, each part carries the equivalent of the whole. This property could easily be present at the energy level of a homeopathic remedy; every single cc would then hold the full energy power of the whole 100cc. There is, therefore, 100 x 100 (10,000) cc of available memory - a hundredfold increase in power.

When the homeopath adds 10cc of a liquid homeopathic remedy to the first 100cc of pure water, there is 110cc of liquid (100cc of pure water and the 10cc of a fluid treatment). Based on the principle of each part carrying the energy impression of the whole, as with DNA and holograms, it is feasible every single cc of the new mixture now carries 110cc worth of homeopathic energy. With 110cc of new liquid now holding 110cc of energy in each cubic centimetre, there is now 110 x 110cc (i.e., 12,100cc) of homeopathic charge.

Those numbers illustrate the principle of escalating energy transfers; they are not intended to be exact measures. However, unlimited power increases through that principle happen every time a fresh 100cc of water receives a shot of the ever-increasing energy force into each cubic centimetre of liquid. The source remedy is being significantly diluted, but the energy power increases enormously every time.

Despite the practical barriers, most of us who work with treatments connected to energies still promote the case for combining complementary techniques with orthodox medicine. Sadly, as my conversation with the consultants indicated, there is no easy route for all kinds of healers, dowsers, and complementary therapists to be accepted alongside orthodox health professionals. Until the world of energies is taken seriously by the decision-makers, the energy sector can only keep giving its account of events which may one day transform healthcare.

As more people worldwide introduce themselves to complementary therapies and techniques, the help that energy workers give to clients will multiply. Eventually, more trained and experienced energy practitioners could bring immediate cost savings to the healthcare budget and considerable improvements in patient care, health, and wellbeing. Our regular casework has many examples to show what it would mean for the health industry to help make this leap. One potential opportunity opened with the news of the sort of scientific breakthrough which gives scientists the popular authority they enjoy. Pioneering surgery used cells from the nose to suggest the possibility of correcting paralysis in cases where the spinal cord had been severed. Amazingly, this approach seems to encourage the nerves to grow again to return movement to the patient; on the face of it, a powerful potential treatment. But from a healer's perspective, the process would deliver much more if the patient's after-care included energy healing.

Surgeons believe that once the new cells are introduced into patients, the body's natural healing processes will go on to repair the spinal cord. One thing we know about the work of healers is their ability to boost this natural healing capability. Binding healing energies into the surgical treatment would increase its effectiveness and assist recovery. Any competent and experienced healer could improve the prospects of success for the treatment and a speedier recovery for the patient. It would be a huge boon to this new technique if it were developed and a significant opportunity for scientists to test the impact of energy interventions in experiments under their control. The prize at stake, a potential cure for paralysis, is well worth serious study.

For now, an immense power available across the universe is unfairly dismissed by those who should be exploring it most keenly. The force which created the universe and developed the complexities of life must be acknowledged by the political, scientific, academic and media channels. Most of those with influence who are not primed to accept interactive energies are not fully helping the society they serve.

The potential of complementary therapies and the practitioners who use them is immense. Television scientist Michael Mosley conducted another televised experiment addressing an aromatherapy treatment which confirmed the oil from the herb rosemary could improve memory. This remedy dates to 3500 BC. Now, in the twenty-first century, a measure of scientific evidence of how rosemary can assist memory has emerged. According to Michael, this property was attributed to the herb in Shakespeare's time. Not only do we now have some confirmation of the power of herbs and the skills of herbalists dating back centuries, but we also have proof of the extent to which we are culturally conditioned to be prejudiced against successful treatments which science has not yet endorsed.

Once we know the relationship between physical, mental and energy interactions, we can find the evidence wherever we investigate our health and physiology. The first human hand transplant did not generate as much public debate as it might. Reactions to the reports were minimal, perhaps some amazement at a surgical enterprise with such life-changing possibilities for patients, but nothing more. However, there are implications that few have realised. It is also all about how our body energy systems operate in a state of awareness that is a vital part of an intelligent interactive combination running throughout all life forms. Body energies need not die when our bodies do. As far as we know, our energies require no physiological sustenance or support and are not living as we commonly know it. Instead, the system can be regarded as distinct but wrapped up with everything in our life experiences and the rest of our physicality. If that physicality collapses around our body energies at death, our energies should survive. This raises the potential for the essence of life to continue beyond physical death and possibly permit communication with those continuing energies through mediums or others sufficiently attuned to do so. It would also offer a way in which reincarnation could prove a reality. Issue 137 of Paradigm Explorer - the journal of The Scientific and Medical Network - recorded that 'in the USA alone there are some 2500 cases of reincarnation sufficiently robust to be included as having yielded evidence making the instances more robust than just folk-tales.'

There are signs to suggest all those possibilities are real. Science now knows that all atoms - with their subatomic particles - do not die but pass on to something else. I was pleased to hear Professor Brian Cox suggesting this in an episode of his television series 'Brian Cox's Adventures in Space and Time.' He stated that possibly the most important truth of reality was how black holes somehow retained information relating to the universe. It was fundamental to the universe that information sucked into a black hole was not destroyed but somehow imprinted in radiation and released back into the universe as the black hole slowly evaporated. He called the explanation bizarre and 'cool' as it appeared to imply that space and time are not what they seem. Although the professor was relating this to gravity - because it was gravity that formed the holes, and that was his theme - we cannot limit the information in the radiation only to gravity. As I say, all information has energy imprints, and all could be stored and released by black holes.

If information is processed as he describes, it raises immense questions. First, about the information itself, in what form can information be driven into a black hole? It is indestructible, but what of its nature? Is it a product of mathematics - but how is it expressed? How does information about gravity or, as another example, the laws of movement translate into something a black hole can receive, fail to destroy but on its eventual collapse, release back - and into what? A universe, a galaxy, a partial galaxy or redefined spacetime which has neither time nor space?

What is the radiation into which the imprint(s) of information is released? Throughout my book and my work, I have referred to energy imprints that comprise everything in existence. It includes all physicality, thoughts, and actions. The professor's account matches my definition of Intelligent Energies and their role. It would reasonably apply to every other factor of the universe, as well as gravity and black holes. All energy information relating to anything and everything attracted into a black hole is held by the universe. That is even more cool than Professor Cox allowed. Both atoms and information have a route back into existence, either as the data needed to begin cosmic physics and life - or as something more fully formed and at odds with current scientific beliefs. It would account for the information I said was missing from the creation of Smolin's daughter universes. We are back to the symmetry of all things - the energies and birth canals of the planet, the cosmos, and all life. Inherited information is passed on to prevent its total loss and to allow it eventually to return. Multiverse theory would have all the information Smolin suggests. It would be a more manageable process if it applied to renewing individual galaxies rather than whole universes, but that is a matter of detail.

None of this is good news for mainstream science. As the professor had to admit, until the 1960s, scientists generally regarded black holes as absurdities with the overriding view that nature would never have produced anything so absurd; he then showed us a picture of one. He wryly commented there ought to be a law against it. If nature was deemed unlikely to have given the cosmos black holes with such essential features, how did they appear? Something beyond nature as it is currently defined must be responsible. Intelligent Energies fit the bill and expose how seriously lacking science has been in its understanding. Professor Cox confessed that scientists still struggle to fathom the mechanics involved in preserving essential information in black holes ready to be released millions of years later.

It is easy to see how damaging it would be to the cosmos for any parts of it to cease to be. It would be vital to preserving the energy imprints of this reality that would otherwise have been lost forever to a black hole. Black holes may have seemed absurd, but they undoubtedly have a real purpose; the same purpose we achieve when we back up our computers. This could also be connected to the error-saving properties of the binary code proposed by Professor Gates I mentioned earlier.

The topic of energies and a world in which information is not lost poses other major questions. Returning to the survival of body energies after death, what does it mean for those medical organ transplants I referred to? What does happen to the energy connections after a person has passed away? What happens when some of their organs are used in transplants and go on living through the different body energies of another person? What does it mean for the afterlife of a body system surgically separated on their death? What are the implications as the donor body energy mingles with the body energy of the recipient?

This is new territory and requires careful thought. The implications for transplant surgery are particularly intricate, so we need to consider the relationship between interactive energies with that in mind. The energy mass, energy flows and energy centres which make up our body energy systems are the key to life. They relate to our physicality. They are not solid like our organs and limbs and the rest of the bits known to medical science. They are nonetheless a significant part of us - alive but in a different way, which is why they are often known as bio-energy. An energy arrangement that cannot be surgically separated.

Our solid physicality is a matter of cells with atoms and subatomic particles. I want to set this into the context of something I mentioned earlier - all matter is made from atoms, which are full of energy. Atomically, they are therefore electrically charged but fundamentally different from our bio-energy body fields, which have a higher vibration carrying energy imprints of our entire being, including our experiences, emotions, thoughts and deeds. Body energies also relate to the charges of our cellular atoms and can pass those energy imprints into our cells and probably into our DNA. Therefore, our physical cells possess something of our lives and personality gleaned from our body energy systems. Those cells, comprised of atoms, can be surgically separated as part of a limb or an organ, and because the energy imprint is within our cells, it remains there and is passed on.

Like everything else in existence, this package of bio-energy working with the receptive physical atoms is also set within the interacting intelligent cosmic field of Intelligent Energies. Energy transfers occur between all three - Intelligent Energies, body energies and cellular energies, in a relationship which enables and explains everything I have been discussing. It is reasonable to assume that all the parts of our known physicality play their part in this three-way arrangement. For example, a limb at the cellular level interacts via its atomic structure with the body energy system to which it belongs, and the body energies interact with Intelligent Energies.

On death, our body energy mechanism leaves the body. How it happens, where it goes and what, if anything, becomes of it after that is a matter of belief rather than evidential; I shall discuss this later. From what we know of energy and the information carried, it is at least very probable body energies are perpetual. This means a limb or organ transplanted into another person retains its cellular structure with its previous energy imprints from the donor's life.

Now, the new host's existing body energy must interact with the cellular atoms of the strange new organ and vice versa - just as would the donor body to which it had always belonged. There will be traces which helped to define the donor when they were alive but are now connecting to the energies of the new person. Transplanted organs are prone to rejection by the new host, whose immune system must be subdued as part of the transplant procedure. It is likely that the central living energy system of the person receiving the organ is part of the rejection process triggered by a clash of energies.

Once the new organ has been accepted, this entirely new mix continues as life within the recipient, paving the way for surprising and disturbing consequences - possibly leaving them open to issues we know little about. There have been controversial accounts of cases where people receiving transplants show different characteristics from how they were before their surgery. They are known to demonstrate ways which reflect patterns matching the lives of the organ donor. Unsurprisingly, the health community has not readily accepted this connection, unaware of how energies at the cellular level can be passed on to the transplant recipient along with the new organ. Energy imprints from the donated organ would be able to access the subconscious and then the conscious brain of the recipient, with surprising consequences.

The apparent failure of surgeons and others to take these possibilities seriously and considerations of confidentiality makes it difficult for researchers to show what proportion of transplants might be noticeably affected in this way. There is still enough evidence to warrant much more attention to a serious concern. Take these cases:

A young gymnast, a staunch vegetarian, was involved in a fatal motor accident. Just before she passed away, she was able to tell how she could still feel the impact of the car slamming into her chest and going through her body. As a registered donor, she was able to help an organ recipient, who later went on to tell how he too was not only experiencing the accident through the same sensations in his chest but, even more remarkably, how he had developed an aversion to eating meat. Having once been a devotee of burgers, he now found they made him 'sick, and just the smell of them made his heart race.'

A 56-year-old university professor reported how, after receiving a heart transplant, he started to experience flashes of light in his face, producing a hot, burning sensation. The donor of the heart was a police officer who had been shot in the face whilst arresting a drug dealer. The professor said that just before the flashes, he gets a glimpse of what he took to be Jesus. Later, the official drawings of the man arrested for the shooting showed him looking like typical depictions of Christ.

An eight-year-old girl, who was given the heart of a young girl who had been murdered, suffered nightmares about the event. A psychiatrist believed she was 'seeing' actual events and decided to pass the information to the police. This included detailed descriptions of the killer and events which the eight-year-old could give. Those descriptions, along with other facts concerning the time it happened, the weapon and the location of the attack, led to the arrest and conviction of the donor's attacker.

William Sheridan, a former catering manager with a poor ability to draw, became a talented artist following his surgery for a heart transplant: his new heart had been donated by a keen artist.

Passing on such characteristics via the transfer of interactive energies extends everything we know about body energies. The scientific view is a reluctance to accept any real connection between transplants and subsequent events. Broadly, it is claimed any influence on donor recipients could be due to the shock of their experiences leading up to and following the transplant, or of their re-evaluating their own lives. Even the effects of medication are put forward as a possible source. None of those suggestions explains how the changes experienced by the transplant recipients reflect the characteristics of the donors.

Again, scientific explanations do not begin to match reality. They confirm how science, faced with challenges outside its models, persists with implausible explanations rather than seriously investigating the truths. One medical theory considers cellular memory as a factor in these extraordinary reports, but cellular memory alone is not enough without the subtle complexity of interactive energies. It is far more likely that the transfer of such detailed information would come from the donor's own energies locked into their cell particles. The energy imprints would plausibly be accessible through interactions with the energy systems of the new host. This may be via receptors in the heart or other locations of the host functioning as contact points capable of receiving the information and generating the outcome effects.

Interestingly, two of the cases above involved heart transplants, which might relate to the concept of a heart brain. As with most energy work, the phenomenon may well depend on how sensitive the donor or the transplant recipient was to energies. This variation would account for those cases in which the new host does not report anything different or untoward after their transplant experiences. In the same way, many people do not recall dreams.

This is not to raise objections to the practice of transplants. But there is reason to suggest those involved in any part of this field should become aware of - and so better deal with - any possible repercussions. Ignoring these possible issues for any reason is a disservice to the donor and recipient and both families.

The topic is full of energy implications which, on a positive note, do include the strong possibility of being able to modify any troubling consequences of a transplant with the aid of energy treatments. These might include hypnotherapy, Emotional Freedom Technique (EFT) and Neuro-linguistic Programming (NLP).

CONNECTING EVERYTHING

'We should take care not to make the intellect our God; it has powerful muscles of course, but no personality.'

ALBERT EINSTEIN

There has been enormous growth in the range of complementary products and services available online and in shops. In this market, traditional and new treatments mingle, and all have interactions with energies. In a newspaper article, British journalist Jan Moir wrote on a topic similar to those businesses which, controversially, enlist the help of dowsers. Jan, a sceptic in such matters, confirmed it was no secret many successful professionals increasingly include corporate spiritual advisers amongst their teams of consultants. The article also suggested that a quarter of the British population have consulted a psychic. Taken literally and allowing for demographics, some 10 million UK adults have contacted people who claim psychic powers, a gift only interacting energies can comfortably explain.

Beliefs have been changing over recent decades, particularly in the west, with the movement away from traditional religious loyalties and towards increased interest in spirituality, energy techniques and therapies. Growth in awareness is welcome, but for those ready to push through the boundaries, finding the best way to explore the potential of new ways of thinking can be challenging. It can be difficult to know where to go for advice or support. Science has its limited boundaries; religion has its specific doctrines, which are a deterrent for some, whilst those who work directly with interactive energies and have much to teach generally do not spread their work to include the wider picture of life and the universe.

Encouraged by my proven healing and dowsing results, I wanted to address this fragmented picture of reality in a cause to establish one set of rules for one shared universe. I began regular visits to Mind Body and Spirit Exhibitions to improve my background knowledge. Whatever topics interested me, I examined more deeply, seeking more and more information from books and magazines and talking to exhibitors. Energy work continued to prove itself, moving me towards the point where the 'muscles' of intellect observed by Einstein gave way to some level of personality. It is open to everyone to explore where all this can take them. Wherever it leads, always consider two strands. One is to recognise the practical prospects of new healing techniques which might help you - and even potential energy skills you may possess without having realised. The other strand is to be prepared to revise your views on life and a planet which works to unfamiliar rules. The key opportunity Intelligent Energies offers is to explore a more connected picture. In *The Book of Life* author Gwee Li Sui nicely summarises the plight of planet Earth waiting to be fully understood in this way when he says:

'What the world is, is a book in a room in need of a reader. Its brown pages have not begun to seed consciousness that joins our senses to another.'

A lovely message which teaches us to see the planet's vulnerability, our heedless onslaught and our failure to understand our responsibilities towards its needs. We are missing opportunities for finding harmony. As Gwee Li Sui observes, there are too few 'reading the book' - our world - as it needs to be seen. Even fewer are reacting as they should, and the Earth waits to inform readers. A plea, again, for more connectedness.

Whilst Einstein's metaphor of a distant piper has not caught on as a realistic overall structure, the time has come for more of us to share his view of a greater purpose. Time for those who find the answers to spread greater awareness of the potential others cannot see. More people are heading this way, and many more will likely follow. The implication of Intelligent Energies on a universal scale is the story ready to be revealed.

I enjoy considering any topic, particularly scientific ones, with the benefit of introducing interactive energies. I once gave myself the task of formulating my own theory of everything based on energies. This is not the one science is looking for, but perhaps it should be. This is what came out of my sudden stream of consciousness - guided by the intelligent universe:

Everything exists as universal energies arising from an interactive source, making everything aware (consciously or not) so that everything may interact with everything else through sentient energy fields.

Everything, organic and inorganic, is driven to build progressive cohesion through interaction, evolution, and adjustment towards a functioning universe.

Everything appears from energy but in forms which are individually unstable. Separately, everything other than the energies is temporary and a matter of individual detail; collectively, there is some permanence, but always changing and advancing.

Everything affects everything else through energies, all thoughts, words, deeds and events. A world within atoms and atoms within matter. Worlds within galaxies and galaxies all within their source.

Sentient beings may choose their definitions, interpretations and priorities, but mostly they must carefully choose their actions. That is everything they cause or create as an individual. We are a part of everything, and everything counts.

The conflict between the ideologies of practical science and the alternative implications of spirituality and energies can be harmonised. It is a balance essential to a full understanding and will belong within any theory of everything. Is any eventual scientific version really going to sustain present beliefs that the whole of creation emanates from chance? General science must eventually adopt something more plausible, more in harmony. A rainbow is a simple analogy to show how differing perspectives need not clash. Whenever we see a rainbow, we appreciate its colour and appearance. It is a pleasant experience we immediately share with others alongside us. We do not scoff at what we know is the myth of a pot of gold at the end of it. We accept it as the sun's light refracted through raindrops.

The website dogonews.com carried an article on 24 January 2016 identifying 12 kinds of rainbow according to the Centre for Meteorological Studies in Toulouse, France. We see them all as light and pretty; science addresses them in more detail. They were used as a symbol to focus support for the UK's National Health Service during the earliest Covid pandemic. From mythology to hard science, none of this clashes or takes precedence. A rainbow is all of them, sharing their place according to context and covering all we need to know.

Looking differently at nuggets from the world of science confirms the concept of a universe working through Intelligent Energies. The standard meaning of any intelligent mechanism relies on brains and conscious understanding. However, sometimes science shows how awareness is present without these faculties. Even garden plants, for example, show interactive awareness. Naturalist Sir David Attenborough included an experiment in 2017 during an episode from a fascinating television series 'Nature's Curiosities.'

Using a sound amplifier, he showed how flowers have an energy field stronger at the head than lower down the stem. We listened to a sound between a whistle and a whine, the tone of which changed as a bee flew close to the energy field of the flower head. The change was signalling the bee's presence and the reaction of the flower. Sir David's commentary referred to the flower having grown out of the Earth carrying a weak negative charge which he said explained the source of this exchange. It seems highly relevant that the stronger field was at the top of the flower, not lower down nearer the Earth where it presumably started but where it would not be as valuable to the bee or the flower. Nature has contrived to choose this as the best arrangement.

There is no doubt an interaction between bee and flower energies was taking place at the flower head. Its negative charge attracts positively charged bees to gather the nectar. Even more astonishingly, pollen 'jumps' from the flower towards the bee during the process. To complete the cycle, the flower then switches off its negative charge, which signals to other bees that no nectar is available until it builds up again. At this point, the negative polarity will be restored. These reactive polarity switches show there is much more to the flowerhead energy field than a benign magnetic charge carried by the original flowers simply growing out of the Earth.

The experiment proves the bee and nectar relationship is way beyond a purely mechanistic one; it also demonstrates awareness on behalf of bee and flower passing messages about pollen build-up through variations in the 'tone' (or polarity) of the flower energy. It also demonstrates the role of energies I advocate, even if science doubts the process involves the intelligence I describe. Sir David, understandably, addresses the forces engaged in terms of the physics known to science. There is currently little else he can do. He also confirms the processes between bees and flowers are not yet fully understood. The effects of magnetism are comfortable enough but do not fully explain how the complex cooperation ever arose or exactly how it operates and controls itself whilst communicating about changing circumstances.

The same programme explained that when under attack from caterpillars, cabbages emit scents which wasps pick up. They recognise the caterpillars represent food and are drawn to the rescue of the cabbages by eating the pests. The same scent also warns the neighbouring cabbages of the attack, allowing them to form chemicals in their leaves which the caterpillars cannot tolerate, so fewer cabbages are eaten. The process benefits the nearby cabbages and wasps but at the expense of the hungry caterpillars. For this performance to be conducted entirely at the physical level is difficult for science to explain fully.

Sir David's programme also observed how the roots of plants could communicate through the medium of sound, perhaps as 'a simple echolocation system' which might help them navigate through the soil and avoid hard objects. The quiet ticking sound of corn seedling roots was recorded, and when played back to them in an experiment, Sir David illustrated how they headed towards the source of the sound.

All of this shows the world of plants communicates by vision, touch, smell, and possibly hearing. The prompts that Sir David was describing match our connections with Intelligent Energies and the energy messages to which we, too, respond - often inadvertently. Humankind, plants, insects and all other wildlife have the same access to these universal inputs, which begin as energy nudges and are translated into actions. For cabbages to release their scent when caterpillars are eating them requires awareness of an invasion taking place but without human levels of comprehension. Even so, the energy alert causes them to release chemicals to warn others and attract wasps whenever their leaves are threatened. The cabbage has no known means to recognise an attack or to reason what to do about it, but the results are just as effective.

Without the help of Intelligent Energies, it is hard

to imagine a purely physical plant world escalating from that state of not knowing into an alert system to attract wasps. By any other name, such interactions must involve a similar system to the bees' relationship with the flower, monitoring nectar levels, and messaging changes to the pollinators. The critical universal path is information from Intelligent Energies being accessed through the body energies of all life forms for them to respond in different ways. Humankind can readily interact through our intelligence and verbal communication skills. Other life forms can adapt to the prompts by reflex actions, which generate essential consequences through body energies, working as part of the plant's life force.

The way negative charges attract or repel is also partly a matter of physics. Electricity is known in nature - electric eels are one example, but how convenient that the principles of negative and positive charges are also adopted into a living relationship between flowers and bees. However, those mechanisms detected by Sir David Attenborough's intriguing experiment are not simply electromagnetic. Life is undoubtedly something more than the present laws of physics can cope with. Because naturalists study life, they are active in events that offer science the best opportunities to relate to energy work. They are the ideal ones to lead a better understanding from which the whole of science will one day benefit. It is not only flowers and cabbages that demonstrate degrees of awareness of what is happening to them and around them. The following extracts from a BBC website should also be considered in the light of other plants working through Intelligent Energies.

Professor Stefano Mancuso, head of the International Laboratory for Plant Neurobiology at the University of Florence, says:

'We did an experiment with two climbing bean plants. If you put a single support between them, they compete for it. The loser's behaviour is interesting: it immediately sensed the other plant had reached the pole and started to find an alternative. This was astonishing, and it demonstrates the plants were aware of their physical environment and the behaviour of the other plants. In animals we call this consciousness. We don't have a clear idea of how plants can sense other plants' behaviour. Plants are much more sensitive than animals. Every root apex can detect 20 different physical and chemical parameters - light, gravity, magnetic fields, pathogens, etc. Plants distribute all along the body the functions that in animals are concentrated in single organs. Whereas in animals almost the only cells producing electrical signals are in the brain, the plant is the kind of distributed brain in which almost every cell is able to produce them.'

The critical aspects of Professor Mancuso's message are that plants share a reaction to stimuli by a process conducted through their entirety rather than the individual communication faculties of a conscious creature. This means: (1) plants can be seen as rudimentary animals, and (2) exchanges between the plant energy and the cosmic energy are entirely plausible as a feature permitting plants 'to sense the behaviour of other plants', as Professor Mancuso puts it. It confirms interactions between energies have been primed from the time plants emerged on Earth and almost certainly much sooner. This is precisely what one would expect from interactive energies building the universe and developing life up to and including humans.

Professor Suzanne Simar, Professor of Forest Ecology in the Department of Forest and Conservation Sciences at the University of British Columbia, says:

'Every tree is linked to every other tree underground, the wood wide web. Through these pathways, they talk to each other and then behave in certain ways.

We grew Douglas fir in a neighbourhood of strangers and its own kin, and found that they can recognise their own kin, and we also grew Douglas fir and ponderosa pine together. We injured the Douglas fir by pulling its needles off and attacking it with western spruce bud worm, and it then sent a lot of carbon in its network into the neighbouring ponderosa pine. My interpretation was that the Douglas fir knew it was dying and wanted to pass its carbon legacy onto its neighbour, because that would benefit the associated fungi and the community.'

Awareness of the wood wide web is exciting for scientists, although they tend to focus on the physical underground structures. They regard the tree root systems as the carrier and ignore the communication and awareness shown by climbing plants and the flower/bee connections which do not have the same links as trees. I have no reason to quarrel with the role of tree roots, but we do need to address a much wider phenomenon of inter-plant communications. These root pathways do not explain how trees, like cabbages, can know they are under attack and are driven to action. There must be some awareness of all those factors for an auto system to take over - one which requires no conscious decision making, just like breathing or sneezing. A response to circumstances affecting the living organism comes into play. The automatic reaction is a consequence of events in a relationship with the surroundings at a specific time. A tree under threat does not release carbon in this way without good cause. A similar vastly complex process causes leaves to fall in autumn. Essential to tree survival, this feature too is hard-wired into their systems, ready to deliver, but only when the tree gets the prompt that conditions warrant it. A dead tree does not behave that way, but like a climbing bean plant, a flower with a bee, or a cabbage under attack, live trees respond to information with an appropriate reaction. Something must know the required responses and be able to trigger the result.

The Professor continues: 'There are so many ways we can use this knowledge. We've treated plants as inanimate objects that are there for our use and pleasure. But we haven't treated them with respect that they are sentient beings. If we can shift our thinking, and change our behaviour, that will then be beneficial for the plants and our forests.'

As in Professor Mancuso's piece, communication must occur in and through an environment that embraces actions and reactions without conscious reasoning. It shows a considerable and sophisticated degree of choice and awareness, operating without human faculties. It demonstrates the presence of a system generating information differently and shows there is more to interactive awareness than we commonly recognise. Nothing suggests we are not part of that same system just because we process it differently. Like all life forms, we have grown out of the Earth; for that reason, we all have DNA and interacting body energies. According to an article on 'The Naked Scientists' website posted on 24 April 2018, 'animals and plants share a common ancestor - a single-celled life form which probably lived about 1.6 billion years ago. The genes we share with bananas would have been present in that ancestor and passed down to all animals and plants alive today.

This does not justify the myth that we are 50% banana, but it does suggest we would not be denied access to the same interactive energy processes as all animals and plants. We, too, are part of this spread of awareness by means which, to be functional, do not necessarily require a brain. The energy fields of bees, trees and flowers are related to our own. The arrangement which connects information to bees and flowers to trigger reactions has the same purpose of guiding every living being. It can reach receptors and make something important happen across all creation. It recognises needs and responds accordingly.

The interactive exchange between bees and flowers cannot reasonably have evolved by one flower and one bee, although each has its life role within it. It had to work on a grander scale. 'The Storey.com' website records how 'beetles, flies and wasps are thought to be the first pollinators, accidentally spreading pollen while feeding on flowers. This set the stage for more complex plant-pollinator relationships to evolve. The widespread distribution of diverse flowering plants 100 million years ago coincided with the appearance of intentional pollinators: bees.' Resorting to the words 'accidental' and 'coincided' will remain essential to classical science as long as it discounts the roles of interactive energies.

I have already referred to the dance used by bees, but looking at it in more detail adds to the puzzles for science about how nature works. The bees' waggling and circling movements specifically illustrate to the other bees the direction of the source of nectar relative to the sun and the hive or nest. It is a remarkable characteristic for any creature to have devised, and one might think especially so for an insect. Science appears uncertain about how it began and how it was able to be used by the original forager as well as those to whom the information is conveyed.

It is not only the dance itself, which is so amazing, but also how the bee can calculate the information it will pass to others. What made it realise the information was knowable and would be helpful? The tiny creature, having buzzed in and out and around flowerheads to collect the nectar, also needs to fathom the exact direction of the nest from whichever orientation it has just reached when it is ready to return. It must also recognise the distance travelled and estimate the levels of pollen.

There are different scientific theories about the practicalities of all of this, but I found little on how it was triggered. One theory is that it started as a means to communicate about a nesting site and evolved into something immeasurably more complex over time. This may seem a plausible development but offers nothing about how it happened. As with plants, there is a level of awareness beyond anything we should expect and beyond that which science can authoritatively explain.

Professor Daniel Chamovitz is the Dean of Life Sciences at Tel Aviv University and the author of 'What A Plant Knows' he has this to say about awareness:

'We cannot talk about plants thinking. We can talk about plants being aware of their environment because a plant is very exquisitely adapted to its environment. There's information being exchanged between roots and leaves and flowers and pollinators and the environment all the time. The plant is making 'decisions' - should I change 10° to the left, 5° to the right? Is it time to flower now? Is enough water available? If you grow a plant with a red light on its right and a blue light on its left, it will 'decide' to bend to the blue light.' [Perhaps a reference to reaching towards the sky?]

'The question is, did it know that it was making the decision? All this information is being integrated in the absence of the brain, which is the incredibly cool and unknown mechanism. We need to understand that the brain is but one amazing evolutionary solution for information processing……..but it's not the only solution for integrating information. We live in a rapidly changing environment - global warming, changes in precipitation, and shifting populations. If we don't understand how a plant senses and responds to its environment and then adapts, we might find ourselves in a big problem 50 to 100 years from now.'

BBC and these authors do not directly endorse interactive energies, but everything revealed in these accounts strongly supports their existence. For plants to have demonstrated how much they benefit from interactions between energies opens new lines of scientific research. As well as DNA, we share many of the same physical elements, including carbon, hydrogen, oxygen and potassium. It is not difficult to conclude that everything also shares a similar body energy interface, able to react to intelligent cosmic energies as part of every physiology. This includes the progression by which, from the start, the cosmos has been structuring itself. The exchange of energy information helped formulate the physical universe before moving upwards through plant life and on towards more sophisticated organisms before eventually reaching humankind. Everything has emerged from that first moment of creation and assembled itself as the immeasurably vast and complex cosmic entity we call our universe.

Our bodies are physical, but they are sustained by invisible energies, as is the planet itself, the whole of nature and the universe. We share this reality in which our spirit - or interactive energy - gives us drive and desire in our lives, but we need our physicality to put them into effect. One is useless without the other, as illustrated by Einstein in his quote: 'Science without religion is lame, religion without science is blind.' For science, read physics; for religion, read energies. This sentiment would probably have appealed to Charles Darwin. Without it, he missed his great opportunity to combine his scientific and religious beliefs. He chose science over religion when he could have had both, and the west has struggled for balance ever since.

Across the universe, the same mathematics, physics, and laws are coordinated by the same interactive energies predisposed to trigger life. Wherever life emerges, it will be nurtured, sustained, and modified through the same driven and interactive evolutionary processes as on Earth. Whatever their forms, the organisms will be helped to make the most of the conditions that are their home. Science is finding many planets which are candidates for life, including some which are very similar to ours. As the ability to detect them grows, we are counting more and more in areas of the sky closer to Earth. The critical factor for science is that to sustain life as we know it, a planet must have water, that magical balance of hydrogen and oxygen gases which occurred after the Big Bang. In the right proportions, their atoms form a liquid essential to our lives. This must have been scientifically ready to happen long before it ever did and even longer before humankind put it into words.

Bill Bryson's book '*A Short History of Nearly Everything*' includes his observations that water does not behave as you would expect if you 'based your assumptions on the behaviour of compounds most chemically akin to it.' He reports how it differs from most liquids because although it contracts as they do during freezing, just before it solidifies, it starts to expand and ends up with 10% more volume. Bill Bryson calls this feature 'perverse', 'beguiling' and even 'extremely improbable.' He also quotes John Gribbin, who called the property 'utterly bizarre.'

Astonishingly, life on Earth only exists thanks to this weird facility of water. As Bill Bryson says, were it not so, ice could not float, so lakes and oceans would not maintain warmth; they would freeze from the bottom up and probably stay that way forever. In his book, he ends this fascinating piece by observing how such a world would hardly have the conditions to nurture life, but 'thankfully for us, water seems unaware of the rules of chemistry or the laws of physics.' With fresh eyes and the power of Intelligent Energies, we can see how this aberrant property appeared.

For water to behave as it does, not as it 'should', is another of those extraordinary coincidences on which science must rely to explain what is otherwise wholly against logic, nature or scientific law. Scientists have no real explanation for these mysterious properties of water. How can an accidental universe endow the essential medium of water with the special features needed for life to be triggered? If we allow personality as well as intellect into our thinking, as Einstein recommends, we can also reflect on life emerging on planets which are nothing like Earth. There are no known limits to what may accumulate. An intelligent universe could make almost anything happen.

On Earth, we know scientific laws have emerged from cosmic foundations, which ultimately led to the evolution of life on Earth. Professor Brian Cox has a well-deserved reputation as an authoritative public communicator in matters of the cosmos and particle physics. Giving a television lecture to celebrities, he described how, by rubbing a diamond vigorously, he caused other electrons in the universe to shift to accommodate the results of his rubbing action. He even introduced this part of his lecture with the words 'everything is connected to everything else.' Though he stressed that this interaction across the universe did not help explain what he called 'mystic healing.'

I agree with his observation. The explanation for natural healing does indeed involve much more than agitating electrons. It requires other related energy forms to join in and complete a cooperative healing encounter. However, for energy workers to hear an esteemed scientist teaching how interrelated universal connections are real enough does reinforce a part of the healing process. For electrons throughout the universe to react to each other suggests the interactive transfer of information and the ability to deal appropriately with it is a perfectly realistic event. Something naturalists might take on board as worth investigating.

The Professor's demonstration introduced a related subatomic principle known as the 'Pauli principle', observed by scientist Wolfgang Pauli. This tells us that electrons cannot occupy the same place at the same time and is another of the weird but essential facts about the universe. Without this extraordinary feature, the universe could not exist as we know it because the principle defines how all objects work as solids. At its most apparent, keeping electrons apart gives us somewhere to stand; if it were not so, objects would pass through each other. If electrons were not kept from being in the same place simultaneously, we would have an unworkable universe.

Professor Cox's lecture caused some controversy amongst his peers - not everyone agreed he was demonstrating the Pauli Principle at all. The discussion is too esoteric for me, but since the experts are at sixes and sevens about it, I will offer my observation as an interested viewer. The principle tells us that electrons must constantly adjust their positions for the universe to continue working. If the conditions expressed in the principle are to be met, an electron must have some way of identifying for itself how and when to react. For example, this natural awareness between electrons must operate under the same conditions as plants. That is a structure constantly at work but with no arrangement known to science by which its rules can be learned or enforced. All are connected and behave in a certain way which also applies to remote healing, whether considered mystical or not.

Science refers to the Pauli Principle as subatomic orbital motions which must follow the rules Pauli identified. The physicists see the practical physics processes and can write equations to illustrate them. They need help seeing the influence of Intelligent Energies, which would demonstrate how the methods are possible. Like everything else, it does not make much sense for this hugely complicated interacting system to be a product or process of chance. Interactive Intelligent Energies must have set up all of this and continued to maintain and monitor it. Science has no such model, yet one must exist. Otherwise, following scientific logic, keeping electrons apart yet together in full coordination originally arose by chance and went on running perfectly with no fathomable means of support. Without interactive forces being involved, it is not feasible. Scientists must better understand powers capable of generating a structured universe.

FAITH AND FACTS

'My religion consists of a humble admiration of the illimitable superior spirit who reveals himself in the slight details we are able to perceive with our frail and feeble mind.'

ALBERT EINSTEIN

In the above quote, Einstein speaks sincerely about 'humble admiration' and the 'superior spirit, who reveals 'himself.' But less fulsomely about our 'frail and feeble mind' addressing 'the slight details.' There is a wider theme to those observations. We tend to regard facts as applying to scientific orthodoxy and faith as a matter of religion. To some extent, those are the cloaks each wears, hiding more than they reveal. But there are facts and beliefs related to spirituality and religion, and there are beliefs within science as well as facts. Biblical Creation is not a fact. Basing natural selection on chance mutations is a scientific theory and, therefore, not a fact. It is a belief like any other. In mid-2019, a research study on dogs sorely tested this belief in chance. It showed evolution and natural selection working in a way that seems to cast doubts on the theory.

The study revealed that our pet dogs, descended from the wolf family, have developed a different facial muscle, allowing them to communicate with humans through expressions that enhance their eyes. These 'puppy dog eyes' are specifically intended to appeal to us. Psychologist Dr Juliane Kaminski of Portsmouth

University led the research and concluded there was compelling evidence that dogs developed the muscle to communicate better with humans.

Also explaining the experiment, Professor Anne Burrows, from Duquesne University in Pittsburgh and co-author of the findings, said: 'To determine whether this eyebrow movement is a result of evolution, we compared the facial anatomy and behaviour of these two species and found the muscle that allows for the eyebrow raise in dogs was, in wolves, a scant, irregular cluster of fibres.' She continued: 'The raised inner eyebrow movement in dogs is driven by a muscle which doesn't consistently exist in their closest living relative, the wolf. This is a striking difference for species separated only 33,000 years ago, and we think that the remarkably fast facial muscular changes can be directly linked to dogs' enhanced social interaction with humans.'

The world's media picked up different aspects of this news, but one message was clear: the development happened after dogs had joined with humans to become domesticated and trained as working dogs. Darwin had an angle on what happens when we domesticate animals and rightly said that selective breeding by humans worked along the same principles as natural selection. That is through manipulating what we now know as genetic changes in DNA. However, in natural selection, the genetic mutations are thought to have become hard-wired by the physical advantages they bring. They enable species to be the most efficient amongst competitors, predators, and prey through the survival of the best adapted.

In selective breeding, the breeders cultivate and nurture the most desired adaptations. The species' evolution is not advanced by prospering through the life-or-death competition for survival in the wild - it is in return for their work or the resources they bring. Their relationship with humans continued as they became pets rather than working animals, but the bond and the dogs' needs changed. Their value as working dogs remained, but new breeds became dependent on attracting and being selected for their appeal and companionship.

Both natural selection and selective breeding depend upon the surprise appearance of an initial, beneficial genetic mutation. In the wild, the entire population of a species benefits from (apparently) one initial genetic quirk encountered by one species member. It provides the critical factor which, over thousands or perhaps millions of years, dominates that population. Whole species face the same needs and opportunities. Eventually, those members with the boosted gene proliferate, and those without it are doomed.

The scientists conducting the puppy dog eyes research are confident changes occurred after the animals had begun to be domesticated. Consequently, no single animal could have spread a mutant gene worldwide. Initially, there was no single population, barely even colonies, just groups of farmers and others scattered worldwide in separate communities using dogs who could not interbreed throughout the entire canine population. For the appealing eyes to spread amongst all dogs, the same appropriate gene had to appear by chance multiple times in different disconnected breeds and various locations across the planet. Interactive Intelligent Energies could facilitate this, but for chance to do so seems impossible.

The facial contact triggered by the new muscle helps bonding and communication with humans. The dogs make themselves irresistible, and we respond. Precisely what both parties need to cement a mutually beneficial arrangement, once established, a conscious or subconscious preference for specific characteristics would enter the selective breeding processes to be continued and strengthened. The principles are the same as natural selection in the wild but not so brutally earned. They spread more from desire and need on the part of dogs now relying on their domesticated status for survival. Such a connection between the best interests of dog and breeder could only be made at the energy level.

It is underlined by another interesting aspect almost hidden in Professor Anne Burrows' account: 'the muscle that allows for the eyebrow raise in dogs was, in wolves, a scant, irregular cluster of fibres.' In other words, something of no use to wolves pre-existed dogs but was ready to be ignited thousands of years later when it would become highly important. That, too, does not suggest a process of chance.

It also strengthens the earlier point that random genetic changes to one creature are less plausible than cosmic Intelligent Energies constantly reacting to needs on a grander scale to make the transition to advancing the species smoother, quicker and more consistent. Much better for the vital mutations to be initially introduced into many members of any species, not just one.

Interactive energies, as the command module for natural selection, generate all the ever-growing, ever-changing, ever more sophisticated versions of all living species. Bill Bryson used the information from science to reach a similar conclusion regarding life. In 'A Short History of Nearly Everything,' he observes: 'Every living thing is an elaboration on a single original plan.' [A reference to DNA]. From this, he also concludes: 'It cannot be said too often: All life is one. That is, and I suspect forever will prove to be, the most profound true statement there is. Concerning science at present, that is a sound observation. However, it is equally true and profound to know that Intelligent Energies are active as the source to make everything happen.

This returns us to the biggest unanswered question about an 'illimitable spirit' to which Einstein refers. The question at the heart of any discussion about fact and faith is whether God exists in the universe. As I have said, we often overlook how God, religion and The Church are three separate concepts leading to beliefs and doctrines which are then applied and sometimes altered by successive Church leaders. Their alterations, decisions and unrequited expectations do not demonstrate no God exists. We cannot make any god responsible for the weaknesses of humankind or deny Divinity because it does not appear to work as we have been led to expect. Spirituality does connect to religion but is not inextricably linked. A dictionary definition refers to spirituality simply as 'the quality of being concerned with the human spirit or soul as opposed to material or physical things.' We can achieve spirituality without embracing a God or religion if we choose.

What exactly is spirituality as a means of 'concerning ourselves' with our 'human spirit or soul'? How is spirituality addressed and expressed, and how does it compare with religious practices? The University of Minnesota responds to the question of 'What is Spirituality?' by suggesting it is 'a broad concept with many perspectives. In general, it includes a sense of connection to something bigger than ourselves and it typically involves the search for meaning in life. As such, it is a universal human experience - something that touches us all. People may describe a spiritual experience as sacred or transcendent or simply a deep sense of aliveness and interconnectedness.'

It continues, 'some may find that their spiritual life is intricately linked to their association with a church, mosque, or synagogue. Others may pray or find comfort in a personal relationship with God or a higher power. Still others seek meaning through their connection to nature or art. Like your sense of purpose, your personal definition of spirituality may change throughout your life, adapting to your own experiences and relationships.'

Further to its observations, the University's text includes statements from leading spirituality voices such as Christina Puchalski, MD, Director of the George Washington Institute for Spirituality and Health. She contends spirituality 'is the aspect of humanity that refers to the way individuals seek and express meaning and purpose and the way they experience their connectedness to the moment, to self, to others, to nature and to the significant or sacred.'

Those who practise religion have much in common with those versions of spirituality; it would be strange if they did not. However, practising religion goes further and perhaps deeper by consciously reaching outwardly through doctrines determined by their religion and church leaders. What connects spirituality to religion is the sense of a greater power beyond us; for the religious, that would be God. It would be something less defined for those who do not practice faith.

In fewer than 300 words, the University appears to have presented the essence of spirituality exactly, though with slight differences. Intelligent Energies add an extra model. A new paradigm which rationalises that sense of a universal power. It guides evolution and knowingly interacts in a sentient fashion with everything in creation. But it is also a driving force with which we can all communicate personally.

I used to wonder if the energy force used by energy workers is the same power interpreted as God by believers until I realised it is entirely possible for there to be both. God may well be another much greater force beyond practical Intelligent Energies. An even higher power in action as the primary source which first gathered Intelligent Energies as a slightly denser, more physical intermediary. It may be that a bridge in the form of Intelligent Energies was needed to enable the lower vibrations of all physicality to reach out more effectively to a much higher force. A stepping-stone to help us understand something of that greater power which had called into being the development of the cosmos and the evolution of life throughout the universe. A power whose followers are entitled to regard as Divine if they wish.

As well as faith, a strong basis for belief in such a higher force reflects the point I made in my introduction, that life represents purpose for our universe. For the active Intelligent Energies to bring order to the ingredients from the Big Bang and to fashion them into a universe, they would have to be aware of their role and what was the intended outcome. Without a clear purpose to guide evolution, we would again be left with only the prospect that everything did assemble mainly by chance, albeit assisted by the 'lower order' of Intelligent Energies. Intelligent Energies might well have been able to create their own purpose by giving it their attention, but then again, maybe not. It does not feel right that the essential Intelligent Energies sprang into being for no reason and with no purpose but then established for themselves that they must now fathom and interactively evolve a cosmos.

There is more depth to the mystery if we address the idea of a higher almighty power that also unites the living world through the bonds of family and parenthood, a moral direction to our lives, empathy and care for others. This is expressed explicitly through spirituality and religion. No perspective has any credible evidence to discount the presence of a God of faith. Sceptics can believe there is no divine power, but that belief is not proven. No belief becomes a fact without evidence.

Scientific discoveries and energy work (or mysticism) are both human evidential activities. They sit at opposite ends of the spectrum of the three historic perspectives defining human experiences. Between the two, we can place spirituality, including a God figure, as a mysterious focus of faith about which we must make up our own minds.

Einstein repeatedly makes references to matters spiritual, religious, and even mystical. It shines in the warmth of his quote at the head of this chapter. He does not say whether he interprets this superior spirit as a divine power or another form, but both would remove chance and coincidence in life and the universe. The presence of some intervening force becomes more and more apparent. Darwin's theory of evolution by natural selection strengthened the certainty inherent in a secular world. That certainty is starting to slip as new theories and discoveries come into view. It is becoming increasingly apparent there is indeed too much complexity in the workings of the universe for it to have relied on chance encounters. The presence of an intervening force backed up by energy experiences is more and more compelling.

Facts about Intelligent Energies and the conclusions which might reasonably be drawn are clear enough. Facts established by science are equally clear, though incomplete, given their failure to accommodate the world of energies. On the other hand, faith differs from known facts because it is not evidential knowledge. That is what makes it faith and is justifiable as such. Those who have faith in spirituality, especially when faced with the challenges of a secular world, should be admired. Separating aspects of fact from faith is almost impossible because whichever belief is held colours what is regarded as the truth.

There are facts to be gathered from the millions of first-hand energy interactions with the sentient forces of the cosmos. Faith is whatever anyone believes lies beyond the facts of those interactions and regardless of how we come to our belief. Intelligent Energies provide reassurance, if needed, for those who are already religious or spiritual and those still searching. Faced with solid evidence that there is at least one sentient, interactive cosmic power makes the presence of an even higher God a stronger probability as well as a matter of faith. If Intelligent Energies can exist, so can God, either as an ancient interpretation of that one immense natural energy force or as a distinct and much greater power that began it all.

However we interpret them, the cosmic energies are powerful enough to have generated our fantastically complex universe. They respond to us individually in ways which invite us to reciprocate. We can interact directly through techniques we conduct for ourselves or indirectly through the gifts practised by energy workers to help enrich our lives. We may act spiritually in whatever manner and means we wish.

Western culture has its patterns, and Intelligent Energies wait to be acknowledged as a common thread to bring that culture together. Governments, academia, health providers and society must act closely and confidently with this thread. It is ready to join together the patterns of scientific truths, energy events and practices, and the spiritual dimension.

Faith and fact are not complete alternatives. We all live with some degree of both and choose how we see life with all the options available. We have the right to find our own way of working with the cosmic forces in whatever way suits us and in whichever belief system works best for us. Science will never prove or disprove God's work, nor can I - and I would not want to. Faith in God is an admirable quality which religious followers should hold on to.

For scientists to take on board Intelligent Energies will enhance their understanding and advance their thinking. As well as Einstein's piper, there is the late theoretical physicist David Bohm's concept of 'Hidden Variables', which I shall address in the next chapter. His work takes a giant scientific step towards greater knowledge that precisely reflects an intelligent universe.

NEW OPPORTUNITIES

'Religion, Arts and Science are branches of the same tree'

ALBERT EINSTEIN

Einstein's quote helps draw together the threads I have been gathering. By combining our three perspectives, each gains by its association with the others. In 'Arts', I include the art of healing and related practices. As always, the obvious potential misfit in those tree branches is that of science, but there is growing reason to suggest this is changing. My work shows Einstein is perfectly justified in his concept of a unifying structure. As modern scientists learn more about life and the planet, they face the gaps in conventional thinking. Experiments and theories show implications that could soon combine new patterns of thought within and between all of Einstein's tree branches, opening vast new opportunities for the world.

Possibly the clearest, purely scientific evidence for interactive energies is known as the Schumann resonance - a natural electromagnetic rhythm of the planet which keeps us healthier and better focused. Sometimes regarded as the heartbeat of the Earth, it is caused when the planet's magnetic field becomes affected by reverberating fields between the Earth's surface and the ionosphere. Scientists know humankind is adversely affected if we are denied this naturally created resonance. For our health to be so dependent on harmonious resonance with magnetic fields highlights our rapport with Earth, energies, and nature.

Scientific experiments have shown that when people spent time in specially prepared bunkers which kept the Earth frequency of 7.83 Hertz from reaching them, their health, wellbeing, and functionality were impaired. Normal efficiency was restored when access to the Earth's natural harmony was made available again - an experiment emphasising how geopathic stress, Earth Fatigue, and electromagnetic fields similarly and directly impose themselves on our health and wellbeing.

This explains our vulnerability to those energy fields with which our body energies are not compatible. It also demonstrates how our body energies do have receptors through which the Schumann resonance benefits our bodies. Recognising the impact of the resonance moves science one step closer to the whole principle of energy fields as a feature of Earth and life upon it. This remarkable phenomenon is much more important than an interesting anomaly. It is a specific pointer to our life in and around energies as part of the structure of nature and the cosmos.

Another example is the Higgs Boson, a subatomic particle which helps to create matter. According to the science website ExtremeTech.com, the discovery of the boson emerged after scientists had already found it necessary to 'imagine a new field which might exist everywhere in the universe.' This necessity became the 'Higgs field'; from there, the Higgs Boson was proposed, identified, and then found. Because of its role in forming matter, the boson became known as the

God particle.

The website then confirms there is even some evidence to suggest the 'existence of multiple Higgs Bosons' but cautions that this idea needs significant further study. Even so, the concepts of a new cosmic field and the possible presence of multiple 'God particles' are in keeping with Intelligent Energies as an active force. The New Scientist magazine of 12 January 2022 took this theme one step further by reporting how scientists at the Large Hadron Collider were wildly excited by subatomic particles, which hinted at what was regarded as a 'fifth force of nature' and 'a new era of physics.' I have long hoped this would herald scientific acceptance of Intelligent Energies. New opportunities for physicists to connect interactive energies to known features such as dark matter and dark energy. New Scientist quotes how these forces keep galaxies from 'flying apart' and 'seem to be driving the accelerating expansion of the universe.' Another balancing act for Intelligent Energies - making them a strong candidate to make up the 90% of the universe science cannot find or understand.

Scarcely a week goes by without an article in New Scientist featuring topics which contradict or confound scientific beliefs and for which I see a convincing explanation through Intelligent Energies. Some reports hint directly at roles for interactive energies like the one by top scientist Donald Hoffman, Professor of Cognitive Sciences at the University of California, Irvine, USA. The New Scientist referenced his book *The Case Against Reality*', a theory which encourages us to think of all objects as data structures created so we recognise something of value to us - e.g., an apple to eat. In Professor Hoffman's theory, the object only exists in its objective form, such as fruit, at that time and for that purpose. The rest of the time, it is a data structure.

This data structure is hard to grasp as a practical reality but is similar to what I consider a small energy field. According to Professor Hoffmann, a data structure can appear as an object as required. He calls the apple an objective reality created by his idea of a data structure. But how does this exchange take place? How does the apple data become recognised as an object? Either the apple data structure itself or our body energies must interpret the physicality of every object in the universe from its invisible data. The most credible working mechanism for doing that is Intelligent Energies. Interestingly, the Professor proposes a similar working mechanism he calls a vast network of interacting 'conscious agents' supporting his data structures. These agents match the energies I regard as the underlying reality of everything around us.

In short, all objects have their material form with energy imprints through their atomic/subatomic structures. The Professor and I agree that objects arise from data/energies, but I know that healing and other processes are also connected to those same energies; all are mingling within the reality we see. For such energy interactions to be raised in scientific circles, as Professor Hoffman is doing, could put us on the cusp of establishing a new way of thinking to be followed up and fully understood.

In another step towards connected thinking,

theoretical physicists have discovered how an astonishing binary code lies at the heart of nature. Professor Jim Gates of Maryland University tells how he and his colleagues translated the physicality of the universe into mathematics. To their astonishment, they found equations showing what appeared to be the ones and zeros we use to prevent computers and the Internet from crashing. In technology, these are known as error correcting codes but raise the question of why and how they could appear in nature.

To discover natural error codes, which Professor Gates describes as 'sewn into the fabric of reality' and which relate to the codes we have devised for ourselves, seems almost beyond belief. It has prompted some physicists to speculate about a computer God or that life forms from the future have created the universe as a simulation. As advanced as this thinking is, it is still inside the box of orthodoxy. It assumes computer codes can only apply to computers and software engineers. Rigid thinking is limited to the belief that whatever we see or discover around us can only have a context similar to human invention. Intelligent Energies developing binary code as their tool are not considered.

Incredibly, binary code was first intuited by Gottfried Leibniz in the seventeenth century. Binary numbering, based on the code, occurred to Leibniz through his Christian belief in creation from nothing. It is an extraordinary connection for him to have made. Even more so as it now physically appears in nature. In an intriguing observation, Professor Gates separately points out that this brings together science and religion, which he says are 'often thought of as adversaries.' So they are Professor, so they are.

Intelligent Energies constantly show themselves in science, spirituality, and mysticism. The intelligent universe has forged direct links to a man who, in the seventeenth century, was inspired to recognise ultra-modern binary numbers as part of the physical and natural universe. Back then, and searching to explain Creation, he intuited the binary role in a way we are just stumbling upon for ourselves. We can only marvel at his ability to have done that. His inspiration shines through as another prompt from Intelligent Energies. How else do we explain how binary code from the Big Bang helps build the universe, passes on to a mathematician in the Middle Ages and 400 years later reappears when developing our computer technology? There is no denying a distinct rhythm to this sequence.

Unsurprisingly, an intelligent cosmos assembling at its energy level requires error-correcting codes. Binary coding stores information super-effectively and could be instrumental in preventing a system for the cosmos from 'unravelling or collapsing' as Professor Gates puts it. It would be an essential tool to ensure a smooth transition through all the billions of stages of evolution. However, we must be careful with this new awareness. If energy states are defined only as a form of physics, we abandon their true worth. As Einstein also said: 'It would be possible to describe everything scientifically, but it would make no sense; it would be without meaning as if you described a Beethoven Symphony as a variation in wave pressure.' We all know there is physics to music through mathematics, vibrations, and waves of different lengths. There are explanations for how chords work and why we hear some aspects as melodic and others as harsh or unappealing. The real appreciation of music goes much further, sensing its beauty and the emotions it creates.

Through mathematics and vibrations, we are given and appreciate a range of different musical styles: rock 'n' roll, classical, orchestral, brass bands, opera, choral and so on. We build a part of our lives around our musical tastes and pleasures, all of which influence us in many ways. The music we choose to listen to can contribute to our mood, our productivity and even our health. Music increasingly shows healing power for those struggling with learning difficulties, mental health issues and dementia.

To define everything by physics alone does take away its meaning. Referencing interactive Intelligent Energies or data structures as subatomic particles would only give us a partial appreciation of their role and contribution. Intelligent Energies offer a stepping-stone to help scientists, agnostics, humanists, and others find bigger truths for themselves. For religious believers, accepting the existence of such a practical, physical power underlines their beliefs. Quantum mechanics form the basis of everything - they do not represent the totality of reality but are integral to it. When I first became consumed by the topic of healing, I constantly came across references claiming quantum physics was strengthening the claims and experiences of healers and clients. It gave practitioners greater confidence in their work, which in those days was more controversial even than today. I spent a long time tracking down exactly why this form of science was seen as compelling proof of what I now call energy work. The effort led me directly to what I realised were Intelligent Energies.

As a science, quantum physics is not easy to understand in detail, and I do not claim to be an authority on its various theories or the debates between experts. I can still bring this esoteric field into my fourth perspective on life and the universe. I offer a practical platform we can all recognise, with energy work displaying Quantum Physics in action. This science is the highest brand of academic research available to humankind. Allowing for energies shown by science to interact brings new opportunities to make real progress towards understanding the full potential of a joined-up universe through theoretical physics.

'Infinite Potential' is a film about the work of theoretical physicist David Bohm. It is also the name of a website which expands on the relevance of his work. Decades ago, he was pursuing the interconnectedness of everything. His research was supported by his feeling for an underlying reality of 'Hidden Variables' as the unknown influence pulling the strings to make things happen at the subatomic level. Einstein described Bohm as his spiritual son, and the Dalai Lama regarded him as his science guru. Three influential people who make a formidable presence and reflect an impressive sense of a fourth perspective.

Modern scientists, including Jan Walleczek and Professor Basil Hiley, are now returning to Bohm's views and the theory of the wholeness of the universe. The biggest hurdle seems to be pinning down that unifying influence, the underlying reality from which wholeness might reasonably emerge. In this regard,

'Hidden Variables' and 'Quantum Potential' are current scientific ideas waiting to be fully formed and accepted. The inspiration is there, but the path is fraught. Quantum theories abound, but they also conflict and serve to split scientific thinking. The flow of agreement within this aspect of science is weak but heading in the right direction.

The concept of Hidden Variables is a possible unifying influence throughout the universe. It promises to resolve the problems between quantum mechanics and Einstein's theory of relativity and takes a step towards a theory of everything. Bohm's paper, published in 1952, argued that 'the motion of electrons were not chance processes' and that underlying 'pilot waves guided electrons.' Put this way, it was too much for the scientists of the day. Robert Oppenheimer, who led a group of physicists exploring these issues, said they either had to disprove the concept or ignore it altogether. There was no way they were going to adopt it. Despite best efforts, scientific orthodoxy could not disprove Hidden Variables and pushed the theory off the table. Not a very scientific approach, one would have thought. Worse still, the ghost of that ignorance seems to have lingered in science ever since.

The outcome was a group concept known as the Copenhagen interpretation, the details of which are beyond me and of little relevance to what I have to say. Professor Dawkins describes it as preposterous, partly because of the improbable consequences which theoretical physicists still argue about. According to Viktor T. Toth, recorded on the Quora website, Einstein also opposed it because (apparently) it implied science could no longer determine exact answers. Toth writes to explain: 'Einstein disliked the probabilistic Copenhagen interpretation of Quantum Physics. More fundamentally, he disliked the notion (as suggested by this interpretation) that physics is no longer a deterministic science: that instead of exact answers, even when initial conditions are exactly known, it can only predict probabilities. His conviction that nature is ultimately deterministic led him to believe that the quantum theory is, at best, only an effective theory behind which lurks a more fundamental deterministic theory of everything. It is the pursuit of this theory that consumed much of his later life.'

To my mind, science can still be deterministic, but only up to a point. Scientists must allow for the interactive fields which affect and make sense of living influences. They must accept we are in a living universe framed and guided by Intelligent Energies and subject to adjustments over time. Science cannot fully determine any outcome associated with any living entity. Determinism must acknowledge this constraint; a dimension perhaps suggested by the Cerne scientists as a 'fifth force of nature' and 'a new era of physics.' I dare to believe all of this would have placated Einstein.

I doubt the outcomes of random chance for the start of life and the universe were any more predictable before those events occurred. They were not even probabilistic in principle, but with modern hindsight, Hidden Variables (as Intelligent Energies) do explain those events and everything that happened; they might also resolve Einstein's doubts. Most interesting to me is the insight of Jan Walleczek when, as part of the

Infinite Potential film, he observed: 'Mystics have intuited this for millennia, but science is now catching up.' In fact, throughout those millennia, we 'mystics' have been working in direct combination with those Hidden Variables. The refreshing new attention now being paid shows the search is on for a twenty-first century version of Bohm's theories, offering further hope of scientific backing for practical energy work in all its forms.

The value of energy connections is proven every day but, until now, not expressed in terms of drawing the mystical perspective together with Quantum physics. Intelligent Energies either relate to or represent the Hidden Variables which certainly need not remain hidden. The evidence for cognizant interactions delivered through Intelligent Energies is just one example of how we mystics have much to bring to Quantum Physics. Wholeness and the connectedness of everything are key to a quantum theory known as colocation, in which objects that appear distant connect directly at some level. Einstein also had trouble with colocation because it implied connections firing everywhere faster than the speed of light. However, Intelligent Energies offer a better rationale as a new underlying reality which includes cosmic colocation without breaching the finite limits of the speed of light.

By showing how Intelligent Energies are at work in practice, mysticism, Hidden Variables, and Quantum Physics take on a practical mantle far easier to grasp than the intricacies of quantum theories. On 19 March 2021, an email from the Infinite Potential website included the following quotes, which illustrate links between Intelligent Energies, Hidden Variables and the barriers of classical physics that face energy workers. The most striking observations in the email were:

'When one attempts to understand the implications of quantum reality the assumptions of classical physics become obstacles.'

'Quantum physics is the description of the smallest things in the universe, the things we do not see in our everyday world of space and time such as atoms, molecules and the tiny invisible particles which form the entire underlying structure of the universe, including ourselves.'

'The relationship of objects is not determined by their relative positions but by relationships existing at the deeper quantum level. Relative space collapses and linear time ceases to be, it's a timeless world that provides us with a glimpse into the eternal.'

'Everything in the known universe emerges from it; everything we are and everything we do is dependent on it.'

There is no better introduction to the reality of Intelligent Energies as an explanation of that infinite potential. At the point of the Big Bang, the universe has been claimed in science to be as small as a soccer ball, possibly a few metres bigger. I have demonstrated how Intelligent Energies are an obvious guide for assembling all stages of that universe, including any prior progression towards the start of the Big Bang and all events after that. Throughout the entire process, it is reasonable to argue that Intelligent Energies were there or thereabouts and integral to the whole sequencing. Their sentient powers would influence, guide, interact with, and absorb the energy imprints of everything happening - just as they still do.

It is illustrative to accept the process up to the fully functioning soccer ball-sized universe and freeze it there. At that instant, scientifically, there is a small universe comprising the potential for all that is known since. Brian Cox's lecture booklet *'Horizons'* also tells us the universe began as 'something smaller than the nucleus of an atom' and, perhaps, a 'vanishingly small part of......a structure known as the Inflationary Multiverse.' The soccer ball is easier to work with. It did not comprise the universe as we now see it physically, but it had to contain whatever was needed for the universe to develop, and at that stage, it is easy to regard it as wholeness. That was the universe - including Intelligent Energies. Nothing was separate, and nothing has separated it since. There was nothing beyond it waiting to join in. This 'everything' reasonably includes the scientific features we know from holograms, DNA and cellular construction, where a whole being is represented in every aspect, including at the energy level.

The tiny universe went on to develop in all its variety, but nothing changes the fact that the soccer ball universe was unified from the start. Its nature is to remain as one, held together by Intelligent Energies no matter how far it extends. This coherent universe immediately began to spread and eventually assume its known physical form. However, that whole form remains present in every single part of it as colocation. Whatever occurs anywhere occurs everywhere as a feature of Intelligent Energies - or Hidden Variables.

No matter how vast the universe has spread, it remains a single mass.

Throughout existence, intelligent Energies and their multifaceted powers are inseparable from every aspect of the cosmos. Through these energies, the whole nature of the universe at heart remains as one essence, connected through its active forces. In this dimension, the quantum behaviour of the cosmos and its energy interactions take place without travelling. Energy access to any particle anywhere in the universe would be instant. An interconnected, collocated, and continuing wholeness means the universe is one combined entity which captures the whole at the energy level.

Paul Howard's film 'Infinite Potential' makes the new quantum perspective explored by scientists very clear. It is also full of fascinating insights. Quantum theorist Dr David C. Schrum records how David Bohm said the universe should be regarded as a plenum [the whole of space completely filled with matter] rather than a vacuum containing stellar objects. Bohm added: 'We should see the night sky as one whole living organism.' He also said, 'every cubic centimetre of this plenum would contain more energy/matter than the whole of the visible universe.' For that to comprise or include the power of cooperative awareness through Intelligent Energies is a bridge to connect wholeness, science and mysticism. There is no requirement for a particle to travel from one end of the universe to the other faster than the speed of light to achieve wholeness. The particles are already connected as that wholeness. Each one has everything. The connection to remote mystical energy treatments is inescapable.

All are branches of Einstein's tree. His reference to the influence of science in our lives is obvious enough. The principles of organised religion are also familiar, as is the value of spirituality outside religion. The arts, too, have undoubted effects on us through our love of paintings, sculptures and music, as well as the impact of the written word, healing and related techniques. All can be partly explained scientifically but have much more to them than their physics.

TIME TO MAKE A DIFFERENCE

'The only thing that interferes with my learning is my education.'

ALBERT EINSTEIN

From the start, I said this is not a textbook but a discussion to explore a thread that runs through all that exists. It changes everything and releases us from the constraints of blind allegiance to orthodoxy. I found a sense of personal relief and freedom by understanding my place in an intelligent universe. That is what I wanted to demonstrate and share.

I have concluded that I do not have the authority to fit Intelligent Energies into science. I can only use my background to make Intelligent Energies apparent to everyone and to fit what I know of science into those remarkable interactive forces. Scientists must become open to evidence from mystical reality and make room for its implications to help the world move on. It is time to acknowledge a greater reality amounting to much more than the familiar view of the physical universe and life itself. My work, experiences, and the cosmic awareness they reveal build that bridge.

Events and experiences appear in many forms, including opportunities for personal advancement, which come to each of us, often more than we realise. They occur at every level and in every field; the critical part is for us to make the most of them. Due to circumstances, it may not be easy for everyone to do that, but wherever there are choices, there are chances. The energies to which we connect are working for us even if the transition from energy to the brain can be tenuous. It can be challenging to synchronise those vast energies with our personal body energies. I have also shown that, fortunately, there are ways to develop and improve connections, raise our sensitivities and receive help to change our lives.

Much material about healing, meditation, visualisation, and related topics is readily available to help us. The options and opportunities are endless; we need to decide what we are looking for and search for information from reliable sources. Intelligent forces are part of our experiences and can be scientifically understood. They are not a separate component of our incredible universe, not something to be fathomed in isolation like gravity, thermonuclear laws, or even subatomic particles. Instead, they are intrinsic to everything that exists, to everything we know and to that which remains unknown.

Creation has grown with and from those energies. We do not just interact with them. We are of them, along with everything else in the universe. It is possible to get a flavour of this by thinking again about the Pauli Principle whilst allowing for Intelligent Energies as the force best able to initiate and control how electrons keep out of each other's way as they move about each other. At the energy level, we, too, are part of that universal movement uniting us across the cosmos.

We interact and communicate both consciously and subconsciously via the intelligent universe. Thoughts, words, actions, and interactions are practical energy exchanges in a cosmic relationship. Following the Big Bang, humankind eventually spread out of the same origins as everything else. The universal energies began to assemble, leading to the laws of physics and the appearance of matter. Creating atoms, elements, stars, planets, colour, light and, eventually, life. All are expressions of one reality from the one source. There is a seamless accumulation from the early energies to everything that has formed since. Those origins introduced every tiny part and every mighty physicality as one. On Earth, the energies manifest as flowers, plants, and fruit, just as they manifest as us and all living creatures. We are all part of this whole - one which has been set up to evolve.

People seem to have an instinctive understanding of this reality, even if they have differing views on how best to interact or communicate with it. Earlier, I mentioned how inspiration comes from working with the heart of the universe. In everyday conversation, more and more of us refer to 'the universe' as a source of help or guidance. We do not specify precisely what that entails, but 'leaving it to the universe' is now a common phrase. Some instinctive part of our being allows for intervention by sources which are there to help. Whether or not we are specific in communicating and interacting with the universe, we all need to recognise and act when opportunities present themselves. The energies lead, but everyone can initiate their own connections.

Even as a metaphor for the unknown or Intelligent Energies, trusting the universe can be good advice. Intelligent Energies will not ignore our needs because of pedantry or our using the wrong labels. They can look after us by any other name, guiding, informing, and enabling us to fulfil our purpose. Sometimes this goes well; other times, the timing may not be right, causing events to move more slowly than we might wish. This does not mean help was unavailable; instead, our expectations and interpretations were out of tune with what was best for the greater good.

The energy connections we can make to universal energies are easily lost or diverted for a number of reasons, be it our free will, limited sensitivities to the potential of energies, the fragility of the connections between our physical senses and the energy fields, or by interferences from words and deeds of our own, or others. We may also be thwarted by other elements of which we know nothing. Even so, the better and more often we tune in to positive energies, the better we will recognise and benefit from their help and support.

Conscious and deliberate interaction helps us relate to the energies and be aware of the guidance we are receiving. It is worth stressing again that the whole of nature has been developed through these energies without any spoken consciousness to express the needs of life forms. Natural selection has always been a matter of successful responses to challenges moved by need and instinct, not by active decisions. Life requires the essentials of sustenance: food, shelter, reproduction, protection etc. All existence has emerged through responses to its varied needs throughout the developing physical cosmos and all life forms.

The more intensely we interact, giving attention to our needs, the more easily the energy forces can assist.

It is interesting to note how we benefit more from working through problems and adversity but learn less when things go well. When they go badly, we instinctively tune in for the universal help we need, and our instinctive cry for help is picked up. The more we do that, the stronger the connections become. This is not to say nothing will ever go wrong if we stay in tune with the universe. It does mean more will go wrong when our vibrations are low and our connections are weak.

The Earth's own internal life energy streams play their part in our growth and wellbeing, but when distorted, they cause us specific harm. The planet's natural resonance is, without a doubt, a part of our body energy function and requirements. Those Schumann experiments confirmed how we can be affected by dissonance, reminding us of the problems caused by geopathic stress and Earth Fatigue, as well as by other electromagnetic fields which are not in our frequency. Our personal energies need a natural, undistorted rhythm. Negative vibrations from any source interfere with our body energies and harmonics. Care for each other, for all life, and the planet raises positive energies and encourages greater harmony.

Schumann's findings about our human dependence on harmonious resonance with the Earth are the clearest evidence scientists have yet encountered to help establish the good and bad effects of Earth's energy fields. It is evidence for which scientists do not seem to have found any use. If they were more aware, their findings could be applied to the issue of how Earth energies in adverse form and electromagnetic fields can work against us. Scientists will change the world when they grasp this and gather the full implications of interactive energies.

For years, scientists and educationalists have struggled to attract young people to pursue the subject as a career. How rapidly might the scientific world flourish if young people were allowed fresh opportunities to progress discoveries through a new dimension of a universe which they know pulses through accessible interactions with Intelligent Energies? Imagine if new science began to allow a new generation to see for themselves and to work alongside the tangible universal forces which connect everything. Exploring mechanisms for practical and spiritual benefits as well as an enriching way to regard life, the planet and the universe - edging closer to the real power of the universe in a personal way. Energy workers, followers of all spiritual paths, and those otherwise like-minded already fit well into this model. Once scientists adopt the theoretical and empirical evidence, they will make that 'giant leap for mankind' they believed had been made with the first moon landing in 1969.

Everyone has personal access to Intelligent Energies. The universe reaches into us with advances in understanding - special insights emerging as flashes of inspiration picked up in the 'eureka moments' which proliferate in science and for each of us in our daily lives. Enormous leaps which seem to come from nowhere have answered individual needs as well as advanced the whole of humankind. A television documentary 'The Genius Factor' once raised the issue of the 'collective unconscious' influencing our lives.

This is not a new concept; Swiss psychoanalyst Carl Jung first described it, but the programme used it specifically to explain scientific advances that occurred to more than one inventor at the same time. For example, two patents for prototype telephones were filed in the USA on the same day: 15 January 1876. One was by Alexander Graham Bell, who gained fame as 'the' innovator and the other by Elisha Gray.

Was this a device whose time had come and was being prompted into reality by a cosmic field available to anyone tuning in? It is not an isolated case; the paper 'Are Inventions Inevitable?' was published in 1922 by William F. Ogburn and Dorothy Thomas of The University of Columbia. One remarkable statistic emerged showing how at least 148 inventions were then already known to have occurred to more than one inventor simultaneously. Half a century later, it was still happening. Bill Bryson records in his book *The Road to Little Dribbling* how two medical researchers, Derek Brewerton in Britain and Paul Teraska in the United States, made the same significant breakthrough in understanding genes simultaneously in the 1970s.

Collective unconsciousness may not have all the answers but sits well as an aspect of Intelligent Energies. However, if we define Jung's concept only as the collective of all human thought imprints, it does not explain anything beyond or before human existence. Redefining it as the consciousness of the emerging universe takes it beyond human influences. It becomes an aspect of Intelligent Energies and their part in the ways of the universe. However, even this account is not the whole story. The universe's consciousness is more than a data bank; it is also a proactive and responsive force. It can trigger those inspirations which more than one person might reasonably pick up on sooner or later, or even at the same time.[5]

Once we consider those principles of personal and universal energies acting in accord with each other, everything is clearer. The cosmic energies continuously interact on a universal scale, connecting with every other energy field, including our own. We can see spirituality as our relationship with Intelligent Energies or with any higher power; mysticism is the application of that relationship, whilst science is an understanding of its materialistic outcomes. Everything belongs within those three perspectives, and for us to recognise that highlights the fourth perspective in action.

Two quotes capture the essence of this whole new world: the first by a sixteenth-century Persian poet: 'When you are lonely or in darkness, I wish I could show you the astonishing light of your own being.' And then there is former Beatle George Harrison's beautiful insight in his verse:

'When truth gets buried deep, beneath a thousand years asleep, time demands a turnaround. Once again,

---

[5] Also recorded in Issue 137 of the scientific and medical network journal is that Jung believed in the reality of 'parapsychological experiences and mystical experiences.' He was 'searching after a method that could unite both physical and spiritual realms into an overall framework where validations of findings from one sphere could be transported from one domain to another.' The journal further noted that Jung nonetheless supported scientific methodology and 'was not prepared to abandon scientific materialism. This a useful reminder that scientific methodology is fine for those things which science can measure but does not leave science free to dismiss those things it cannot measure.

the truth is found' The truth has been around forever. It has taken many forms and has had many interpretations. Though vital ancient knowledge is indeed 'buried deep', it shows itself in our experiences, regardless of how we account for them. My ordinary, common sense view of the universe was transformed when I found healing as one part of the universe's truths. A nudge from cosmic forces revealed this power and inspired my journey to find the threads. It released my potential to be a healer and, more importantly, to deal with the adverse Earth energies causing huge global difficulties. In 'Haunting and the Psychic Ether Hypothesis', H.H. Price said, 'We may safely predict that it will be the timidity of our hypotheses, and not their extravagance, which will provoke the derision of posterity. Mainstream science and academia should be embarrassed by Intelligent Energies and quantum physics as we await that final straw to bring an end to this poor old materialistic camel.

Meanwhile, those mysteries still swirl around in those mists of their own making. We are told the Big Bang is now regarded by some as discredited, whilst the earliest phase of the universe could be as tiny as a proton or as small as a golf ball. Then it might have been as large or larger than a soccer ball. I have no wish to quarrel with any of that. Undoubtedly, those hypotheses are as 'extravagant' as H.H. Price invited and none more so than Intelligent Energies.

If space did not exist until the universe began to open, the most likely influence would need to something that would not have to take up space - Intelligent Energies, of course, but what about something more extravagant? Since everything has its own energy imprint, what about the fields we regard as abstract? Influences such as awareness, consciousness, knowledge, thoughts, and intelligence exist outside the physical. Any source to trigger, guide, and develop the universe would require those abstract qualities to interact. All have an impact we recognise through our experiences and faculties, but that is not necessarily the only way they have an effect. All our words are abstract; they are all formed from letters and make sense if we read them, but they also turn up in thoughts with no physical image. Testing how the body energies of others change according to whether they feel happy or sad showed how thoughts produce physical effects.

There are so many unanswered questions for science that it is not safe to assume these abstract concepts have no role in establishing the universe. When I recognised this, I recalled how theologians struggle with the meaning of that famous phrase from the Bible - 'in the beginning was the word and the word was **with** God and God **was** the word.' I started researching this and learned that 'word' had been translated from logos which also means knowledge. Replacing 'word' with 'knowledge' makes a fascinating difference. The first source of the universe is then pure knowledge. This knowledge and this source are seen as God, but that knowledge I call Intelligent Energies is also with (i.e., working alongside) that higher source.

Decades ago, removing geopathic stress whilst introducing healing made all the difference to my daughter's needs. I did not set out to become a healer or an author who would challenge or seek to assist scientific eminence. I just wanted to help her. She still has learning and development difficulties, particularly with word-finding, but boosting her body energies brought out her potential. She has since proved to be intelligent, with a great sense of humour and a love of dance, sport, art, and craft. Despite her continuing issues, she can now communicate effectively with us and is a joy to be with. She has blossomed beyond anything we could have expected and is achieving far more than would have been possible had geopathic stress and her body energies remained blocked together as they once were. Removing her shackles was a massive 'turnaround' in our understanding, which might have easily been missed.

Instead, the truth, which had indeed been 'buried deep', burst into our lives. Although their presence was unknown to me then, Intelligent Energies were in action. They connected us to the help waiting to be found. The events which followed led me to a wider purpose along a path seen more clearly with hindsight. I found an energy roadmap which made a life-changing difference. We are all open to developing our relationship with this almost unimaginable intelligent cosmic force. There are many ways in which the connections have been addressed by humankind over thousands of years and many means today to help us interact. The direct relationship is much more than a belief. The practical energies have always been with us as a primaeval matter of fact, now brought up to date for the twenty-first century. Intelligent Energies are one constant, creative and supportive force available to us in our daily lives.

Whatever our present perspective and background, accepting the role of energies becomes a personal opportunity to make our own difference. Enabling us to reach out and embrace a world in tune with the power to spread and attract vital positive reactions across the planet. A planet which needs help to reverse the damage we have been causing and from which we, too, are now suffering. Adopting an active fourth perspective is now imperative and must be our aim. We still have no scientific blueprint or even an energy one for this, but that is not a problem. The Intelligent Energies do not follow our blueprints; they evolve what is needed whilst we play our parts.

We can already see changes in attitudes slowly building towards what will become that fourth perspective. The pieces of new consciousness are in play through the raised awareness of complementary therapies and techniques, the concerns about the planet and the wider acceptance of something bigger than ourselves. Famous names and influential figures in the Arts and other fields often add weight to these themes. Highlighting the presence of Intelligent Energies will provide a tangible focus for their voices. An identifiable brand around which those who are like-minded can gather.

His Majesty King Charles showed his commitment to the environment as the Prince of Wales. He also strongly supported the integration of orthodox medicine with complementary techniques. As King, I hope he can remain true to himself and still support these principles. Greta Thunberg has reached the world's ears and conscience on environmental matters.

So has Sir David Attenborough, who is changing attitudes to plastic and wildlife. Manufacturers and retailers are beginning to listen and modify their ways. The Heartmath Institute focuses on humankind and the entire planet through its Global Cohesion Initiative. Enlightened farmers in agriculture and livestock, as well as other growers, are seeing a better way to work with nature in a new approach recognised as regenerative farming. Like the international Scientific and Medical Network, the RE Fetzer Memorial Trust also supports advances in Quantum understanding and firmly acknowledges a spiritual dimension.

This new consciousness is open to every part of our twenty-first century culture. One day individuals and organisations will become a part of it, but we only have a little time to make that breakthrough. The media must commit to it, as must science, academia, government and every one of us, in our own best interests and those of a desperate planet. Help, inspiration, and answers are available once we join forces - quite literally. Intelligent Energies guided the universe to its ultimate purpose of reaching intelligent life. We are responsible for fulfilling that purpose, not destroying it by continuing to wreak havoc on our home planet, with untold consequences across the galaxy where everything interconnects and spreads as energy imprints.

We make indelible marks on the planet and across the universe through interacting energies. We must learn to make only marks we can be proud of. The fourth perspective will happen, perhaps slowly, as humankind connects and then fully respects the Earth in our daily lives. The Big Bang still represents the apparent start. Now we are in sight of the Big Beginning when humankind understands how our place in the universe is to help fulfil creation. The essential finale for the whole process to be complete is for creation to be understood, appreciated, and fulfilled by the life it has evolved.

My introduction to this book referenced a cosmos of sterile, stellar objects in the vacuum of an otherwise empty universe. I have gone on to show how the universe is not at all bleak and does have a purpose. Finding the true meaning of life has confounded cultures for thousands of years, but the simple answer is that it is all about growth. About a universe growing out of early energies and growing the power of interactive awareness to guide the cosmos. Evolution continues that momentum, developing and spreading species as part of the cosmic process.

It has led to humankind's place on Earth and our responsibility to enjoy, appreciate and nurture what has been created. To represent its magnificent beauty and fulfil the whole purpose of the cosmos from the very start.

THE FINAL CHAPTER

'Light is what you are! It is not something divorced from you: it is you.'

ALBERT EINSTEIN

This quote seems to have Einstein's ring about it - hardly surprising, but for the fact that it is something he channelled after his death. In the same session, he also said, 'the practical applications of channelling are such that would amaze even myself had I been born in your time.'

The observation was not made to me but to Joanna Helfrich, psychic and author of *'Afterlives'* comprising *'Firsthand accounts of 20 notable people'*, and from where I have taken the quote. All those featured are now in the final chapter of their former lifetime, though still learning and progressing with the possibility of other lifetimes to come.

[In an interesting sideline, the computer just started to play up, and I found it difficult to keep what I had just said in print; it kept disappearing. This made me realise I had not asked permission from those I intend to introduce into this part of my book. I also realised that quoting bits from Joanne's narrative does not do justice to what is being revealed in the detailed and sincere messages those who have passed on wanted to convey. I immediately apologised and was relieved to find the computer suddenly working as usual.]

The experience of having my work interrupted in

that way brought me much closer to the sense of the afterlife I had begun to glean from Joanne's book. I now realise those who had given their accounts to her were now looking over my shoulder. Although I do not have Joannes' channelling skills, those good people were in touch with me, and I needed to respect them and their new dimension. I felt I had belatedly gained permission to express something about how the afterlife appears to me, my interpretation of what we might expect when our final chapter is reached. I urge anyone who wants to be fully informed to read Joanne's book.

Throughout my book, I have reflected on all sides of opinions and arguments relating to science, spirituality and mysticism. For me to add my balance of experiences and events generated what I see as the fourth perspective. Joanne's work is part of that bigger vision, and '*Afterlives*' is an amazing read which paints a beautiful picture of life after we have passed. I am indebted to her and those with whom she channelled for the extra dimension they gave me to what I thought I knew.

It had taken me many months to decide whether to address this whole topic of life after death because it is yet another giant step to be faced by anyone still steeped in materialist scientific thinking and maybe a step too far for the message to be received properly. I decided that if it cannot appear in this book, after all the groundwork I have laid, where can it appear? When will the message be received? When can we be open to higher realities?

At some time, we have probably all had some cause

to wonder about life after physical death. Before I had read 'Afterlives,' I had some experiences beyond my healing-energy events, which have given me the confidence to assert that a new dimension is indeed awaiting us. My late father, channelled by a medium Pat Baker, asked why I was not wearing his ring. Nobody could have known I did have dad's ring at home, so this was a significant message, but even more was to follow. Pat told me that dad would touch me on my shoulder, and I would feel warmth. I sat waiting for a sensation of gentle heat at the tip of my shoulder, the top of my arm. Instead, the touch was much further along at the apex of my neck and shoulder and more where a father might touch his son affectionately. Also, the warmth was not as I had expected - it was much more spikey, more like sunburn. The whole wonderful experience had not depended on any input from me - not even wishful thinking. I had no doubt it was a genuine meeting with my departed father.

I had not given any thought to the broader context of how the souls or spirits of those who have passed on spend their afterlives. We know stories about the appearance of ghosts and spirits, but they are all short encounters, popping into the lives of those fortunate enough to receive them. Outside of these brief encounters, most of us probably never consider what experiences those who have passed on are having in their new dimension. It was an absolute treat for me to read Joanne's book with its insights into that world.

There is a common assertion that their non-physical form is regarded as a continuation of their former selfhood. They have advice for us; like the rest of us, they can get angry about politics and even argue about whose turn it was to speak with Joanne. There are mentions of lifetimes they could choose to visit and great concern about what we are doing to the planet. The concern for this topic from the afterlife is particularly telling. Their warnings of consequences if we continue to disregard the reality beyond the scientific materialism (that the more enlightened amongst us are advocating) must be heeded.

A sense of place in the afterlife ranged from having homes, meeting with visitors, having relationships, exploring other dimensions, and even to acting as a creator force. I get a sense that, to some extent, we continue to reflect our Earthly selves but, at the same time, can learn much we did not know before death. I feel those who had some connection with a higher plane during their lives are at an advantage and will make more of their afterlives - perhaps preparing for reincarnation.

Above all, although they are in another dimension, they are just as alive as when they were physical and can be with their loved ones from those physical lives whenever they wish. Their existence perhaps has a dreamlike quality - when we dream, we are in a different reality from wakefulness, but it is just as real. In dreams, we can see, converse, feel touches, eat, move around and play sports. We can recognise aspects of our daily lives, but it is not in the heavier setting of our conscious physicality. Our dreams tend to be short sequences where we are free of the long-term daily plod faced when awake. The most significant revelation with enormous consequences is that conscious existence not only escapes death but is also potentially infinite. I have no means of knowing where this path leads, but it reinforces my commitment to raise all the awareness I can that we must all wake up to the truth.

One of Einstein's most famous quotes is, 'God does not play dice with the universe.' According to the Livescience website, Einstein later modified his observation to 'God tirelessly plays dice under laws which he has himself prescribed.' Livescience points out that Einstein was arguing 'quantum particles must adhere to certain rules that don't change randomly' and that 'the quantum world required better explanations for particle behaviour.' It still strikes me as an odd way for Einstein to make his point. He is still referencing God and, whatever he means by God, has not left particles subject to random chance. The only conclusion to be drawn from this is to confirm that if rules are set for particles, they are set for everything that follows.

With 10,000 others, all keen to learn everything they could about the universe, I saw Professor Brian Cox giving his '*Horizons*' lecture on the nature of the cosmos. I was amazed that such a sell-out audience was willing to tackle what we all knew was a profoundly technical topic. It is fair to say we were all enthralled by the performance, but very few were better informed by the end of it. The professor has a brilliant mind and, without a doubt, is a great communicator, but the way science explains its knowledge of the universe is beyond the grasp of those not within that fraternity. The evening showed the audience was, in fact, buying into hope. We were all hoping to understand how the universe works and how we fit within it. Because the show lacked the input of Intelligent Energies we did not get that clarity.

The brilliance of Einstein was that he was alert to higher forces but also recognised more about the real nature of space-time and gravity than anyone before him. His mind was such that he could measure and write equations about what he knew and forecast the existence of black holes. The consequence of this is that when the black holes were discovered, it confirmed Einstein's genius and helped convince scientists that they did indeed know what the universe was about.

This progress, however, needs to be set into context. To measure, explain and draw implications from the universe we see around us does indeed reveal the results of creation. Science is now measuring the outcome but not explaining how the results came to be. Still, no account is taken of Intelligent Energies or any other guiding force to have influenced whatever scientists are measuring or proposing. All the puzzles remain.

The first paragraph in the booklet on sale at the Horizons lecture said there was only one interesting existential question: what does it mean to live a small, finite life in an infinite, eternal universe? In a way, that question is misplaced; my book and the work of Joanne Helfrich indicate we do not have small finite lives. All life is richer than anything science can measure and deeper than anything for which it is searching. Of course, the work of our brilliant scientific minds is worthy, but it is still one-dimensional. The hope of understanding our universe and our place within it will not be satisfied until the true nature of an intelligent universe combining science, spirituality and mysticism is realised. We have yet to see how long it will take to loosen the deadly grip of materialistic science and move our worldview to the urgent need to rescue life and the planet. To open *'The Intelligent Universe Revealed'* is to reach into the simple yet profound evidence to show how to fulfil our purpose.

Acknowledgements

I could not have reached the level of understanding and been able to help thousands of people without the support I have been given over the decades. Beginning with family and friends, my ever-growing list of clients and their testimonials gave me the confidence to challenge orthodoxy and to commit to a new way of thinking.

As soon as I did, the evidence and the implications became a flood of greater knowledge I can now share. I am grateful to all those who have been and still are part of that process. Special thanks to author and journalist Rosie March-Smith, who guided me as my editor, mentor and friend.

Organisations including the British and the American societies of dowsing, the Scientific and Medical Network, Infinite Potential and The R E Fetzer Memorial Trust share my perspective and gave valuable assistance to my aims.

Others have unknowingly helped by making their expertise available to all of us in ways which helped me appreciate the complexity and beauty of nature and the cosmos. The input of those quoted and referenced throughout my book, as well as others not specifically identified, has been vital over many years. They have highlighted facts and saved me from embarrassment, but they have also helped me expose the dimension missed by science - the dimension of the intelligent universe.

About The Author

Jeff Jeffries was born in Oldham, Lancashire, in the UK. He lived a few hundred yards from the senior school where Professor Brian Cox was educated. A fascinating overlap between two fellow-Oldhamers, who both know so much about the universe from their different perspectives.

Jeff has spent 30 years as a healer, dowser and author. In search of help for his daughter's learning difficulties, he discovered how Earth energies become distorted to affect the health and wellbeing of humankind and all other life forms. Committed to overcoming these distortions – starting with geopathic stress - he developed his technique for clearing them.

He took early retirement from his career as a senior civil servant to become one of the world's foremost authorities and practitioners in his field. His aims now are to help the planet, benefit clients worldwide, and spread the story everyone needs to hear.

Printed in Great Britain
by Amazon